Money Mastery

Creating a Life Without Debt

Marie Beausoleil

Author of

A Cabin Full of Food

and

Going Herbal

Money Mastery: Creating a Life Without Debt

LEGAL NOTICE

I have worked to be as accurate and complete as possible in the creation of this book, notwithstanding the fact that I do not warrant or represent at any time that the contents within are accurate due to the rapidly changing nature of the internet, the financial world and … the world in general.

Normal English: I have done my best, but the world changes fast, so some information may become inaccurate!

I will not be responsible for any losses or damages of any kind incurred by the reader whether directly or indirectly arising from the use of the information found in this book.

This is not intended for use as a source of medical, legal, business, accounting or financial advice. This book is based upon my research and experience, but I am not a professional. Please seek services of competent professionals in the medical, legal, business, accounting, and finance field when making decisions based upon any book, blog post or online course. The reader assumes responsibility for use of information contained herein. I reserve the right to make changes and republish this book without notice. I assume no responsibility or liability whatsoever on the behalf of the reader.

And now that I've covered my butt – I hope you find this all very useful and helpful.

Marie Beausoleil

justplainmarie.ca ☐

INTRODUCTION

You're so very tired of being broke, aren't you?

Ten years ago, EJ and I sat in our subsidized apartment, counting pennies so that we could get the bus to go down to the welfare office.

Yes, it was that bad.

I hadn't been diagnosed yet with brain cancer, and that monster was still in my head. He still hadn't had his autism diagnosis, so he struggled with holding a job. Life was pretty awful in many ways.

That's not our reality today.

We have four young children at home, and we live in a 130-year-old home that we're gradually restoring to its former beauty. We drive nice cars and we don't hunt through the couch cushions for change anymore.

Have you ever thought about the fact that in school, we spent years learning about science, language, math, and social studies from text books, but we spent very little time – if any at all – on real life skills like saving, making, and managing money. It doesn't seem right, does it? And of course, the effects of that lack of education in money shows up – so many people are overwhelmed by debt or are barely keeping themselves afloat.

Somehow, we're supposed to just "pick up" how to manage our finances, as if innate to us! The truth is, money management is not a skill that we're all born with – it's acquired. Even people who seem to have a natural skill with money learned it from somewhere.

I'm not a money expert. I'm certainly not an accountant or anything like that. But what I am is a woman who has gone from poverty to security, from a geared-to-income apartment to purchasing my dream home, from debt to ... well, not debt!

In this book, we'll go over several key areas including:
- Creating and staying with a budget
- Cutting expenses without sacrificing your lifestyle. It is possible to live well without spending beyond your means.
- Saving money every day because if you madly save over a short time you won't have nearly the amount as if you save regularly
- Getting out of debt because it's impossible to build a mountain while you're still filling a hold

- Boosting your income to make it even easier to save
- Refinancing your mortgage – or if that's even a good idea
- How to check your credit rating, fix any mistakes and boost your credit score
- And finally, how to protect your identity

There's a lot to cover. Take the time to answer these questions and implement these steps. After all, your financial success is up to you!

We have a lot to cover so … are you ready?

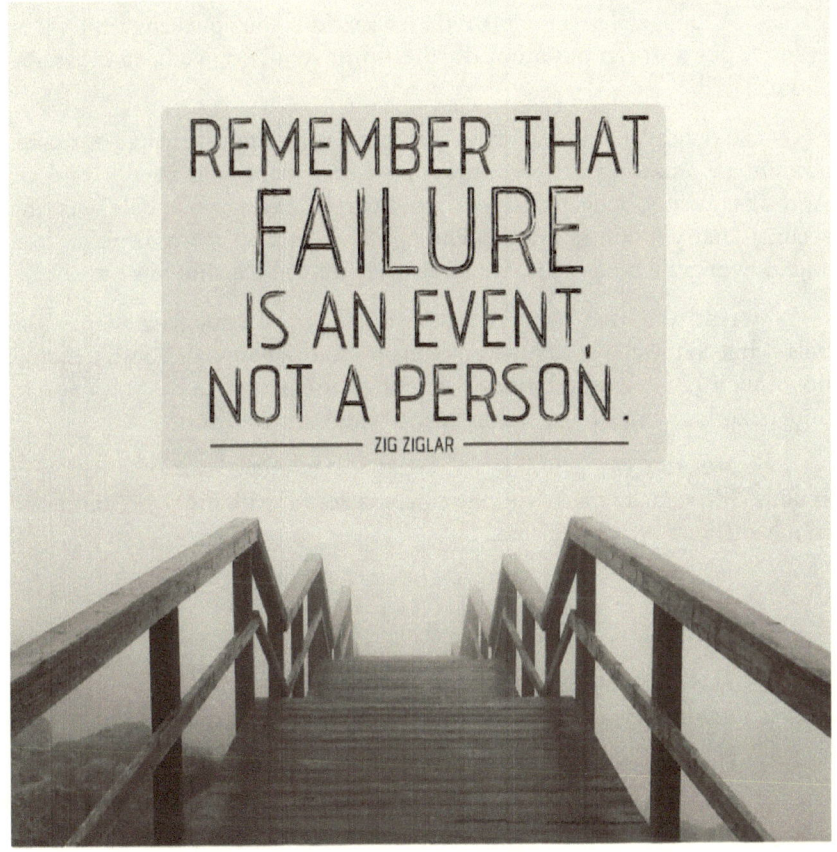

REMEMBER THAT FAILURE IS AN EVENT, NOT A PERSON.
— ZIG ZIGLAR —

CREATING AN EFFECTIVE BUDGET

It sounds almost too simplistic but the best way to have financial security is to have a sound budget.

With a realistic budget, you can have more money to **build that barn** or **buy that new farm truck** or put in **a solar array** to get off grid.

A budget lets you plan that **vacation** you've been wanting or even … put **a down payment on the homestead** you've been dreaming about.

To indulge in these expensive items without destroying your bank account or amassing far too much unsecured debt, you need a budget. And of course a budget lets you live securely, paying your bills with the security that you are not overspending. There are so many benefits to a sound, workable budget that it's clear every household should have one.

And yes, that even includes you if you're struggling to pay the bills while on welfare or unemployment or disability. It doesn't matter how much or how little money is coming into your house – you need to understand how much is coming in and where it's going out.

Not to worry, though! Creating your budget is not as bad as it sounds. It's actually pretty simple. There is some work involved, but none of it is difficult or complicated.

The first question you need to ask yourself is:

How Much Do I Make?

The backbone of any budget is based on how much you make. What's the number on that cheque you drop into the bank.

Hey – a quick aside! I'm Canadian, so it's normal for me to say cheque instead of check. I also use words like honour instead of honor. (Like "You should always honour your financial commitments.") I've been known to do other weird things, too.

Even if your income is lower than you'd like, you can still budget successfully, but it's important to know what you must work with to create a balanced budget.

When budgeting, it's critical that you use your net income as opposed to the gross.

No jokes about how your entire income is kind of gross, please. Right now, your income is what it is. Ignoring it won't make it magically increase, so you may as well take a good hard look and understand what's going on.

Your **gross income** is everything that you earn, including the deductions and taxes that you never even see. There's no sense using this as the start of your budget, though, because it's unrealistic. You might be grossing $2000 a month, but payroll deductions drop it down to $1400 or less. Your gross income is useful when determining your taxes, but it's not very good for determining your monthly budget.

Your **net income** is known as your take-home pay. It's the amount you take home, the amount that lands in your bank account to pay your bills and expenses. This is the amount you are going to be working with.

Again, I want to make it clear that anything **deducted from your pay cheque** is unavailable to you. You can't include that money in your budget because you never see it. Even if you know you are overpaying your income taxes and will get a refund, the money is not available for you to spend. If you get a refund, treat it like a bonus.

The BEST plan (and what we personally have done for years), is to have your taxes set up so that you receive as small of a refund as possible.

No refund? People think I'm crazy when I say it. In fact, we have it set up so that we have to PAY every April.

Why is that? Well, pre-paying your taxes means that you are giving the tax department an interest-free loan all year.

Have you ever noticed that they never put interest on the money they pay you back, but they sure charge interest when you owe them?

By the time you finish this book, you should be financially savvy enough to keep your money in your own bank account, earning interest, so that you can pay the government just what you owe them and no more.

I love my country, but not enough to give the Canada Revenue Agency and interest-free loan!

Ok, so what if you have a **variable pay cheque**?

Well, a close estimate should be good enough in most situations. A realistic estimate can be gathered by totaling your income from the past 3-6 months, and then divide by the income you received in that time.

WHAT ARE MY FIXED EXPENSES?

There's no way around it; we all have bills to pay.

Some bills vary from month to month, but there are others that are constant. Many loans are structured so you pay the same amount every month.

For example, your car or home payments are fixed expenses and you likely know exactly when they come out. Rent and cable bills are also usually the same amount every month. These are expenses that you cannot easily change or eliminate.

Some examples of common fixed expenses are:

- Mortgage or rent (should be no more than 30% of income and preferably less)
- Car payments
- Car insurance
- Property taxes
- Home insurance
- Loans and lines of credit
- Savings (10% of income, or more)
- Insurance payments (car, house, health, life) should be less than 5% of your income.

All told, your fixed expenses should be **no more than 50% of your income**.

Take some time to make a list of your fixed expenses and total the result. These are very important. It may take a bit of digging, but these are usually the easiest expenses to itemize.

If you pay insurance or taxes annually, divide the amount by twelve to get your monthly payment.

WHAT ARE MY VARIABLE EXPENSES?

This is where making a budget gets a little bit tricky. Not every bill is the same amount every month. You don't always spend the same amount at the grocery store or on gasoline. It's easy with the fixed expenses, but here there is room for error. Use an average amount of each variable expense for your budget.

The good thing about variable expenses is that you can change them.

As you'll see, reducing these variable charges is a great way to keep more of your hard-earned cash. In fact, many of these variable expenses can be budgeted and turned into fixed monthly expenses – which will make your life much easier in the long run.

Some examples of common variable expenses are:

- Car maintenance
- Gas
- Food (15% of your income or less)
- Electricity
- Heating
- Phone bill
- Debt repayment (no more than 15% of income)
- Utility bills (electricity, heating, water, phone, internet) should be **no more than 10% of your income**.

Try to keep the total variable expenses to less than 30% of your income.

Take a few minutes to list your variable expenses and total the result.

A good strategy is to go through your recent credit and debit card purchases to see where your money is going.

If possible, try to find a year's worth of these expenses. Yes, this is the hardest part of your budget. If you cannot find a year's worth, then work with what you have.

Your goal is to come up with an amount, even if it isn't exact, that you are spending each month on average for each of these expenses. Utility companies will let you know how much you have spent with them over the past year – divide that number by twelve to find the monthly expense.

WHAT ARE NON-ESSENTIAL EXPENSES?

There will always be things that we want, but don't necessarily need. These types of purchases fit into the non-essential expenses. The difficulty here, is that we often confuse what we want with what we need.

Unfortunately, this is where most of us get into trouble with our finances. We feel as though we need new clothes, a restaurant meal, sale items and much more. One way that I've learned to recognize these non-essentials is if I find myself using the justification that "Well, I deserve that!"

My friend, what you deserve is to live a life of abundancy and security instead of worrying about debt and unpaid bills.

Some examples of non-essential expenses are:
- Clothing and shoes more than the necessary ones
- Entertainment (i.e. DVDs, movies, books, magazines)
- Upgraded computers and electronic devices
- Video games
- Eating out
- Jewelry
- Make-up
- Gift purchases
- "Stuff" you buy because it's on sale

Make a list of non-essential expenses and their total.

Ask yourself: Do I need everything on this list? Is there anything I can cut out without losing the lifestyle I desire?

You are not cutting them yet, though. The purpose in all of this is to understand where your money is going.

WHAT ARE MY TOTAL EXPENSES?

Write down all your fixed, variable, and non-essential expenses and add up the total.

This total will be your base expenditure for the month.

At this point, look at your income. Does it cover all those – plus an amount for savings (if you haven't been saving)? If you make enough to pay all of these and you're still struggling with debt and unpaid bills, then you need to go over the expenses again and figure out where the money is going.

This is an exercise for you alone. No one else sees these numbers unless you share them, so there is no need for secrecy and "fudging" the numbers. Be honest with yourself and look at where your money is going.

If you do not make enough money to cover all of those, then you first need to look at the non-essentials. If the rent or mortgage is not being paid, you simply cannot be going out to restaurants to eat. If you owe thousands of dollars to the gas company, you need to pay that off before winter, and before you buy another DVD – even if did come out of the discount bin.

Non-essentials are called that because you honestly do not need them. I recognize how hard it is to look at something you really and truly want, especially something that will make your life easier or more pleasant, and acknowledge that you really do not need – and should not purchase – that item. I have been there, and I understand.

EARN MORE THAN YOU SPEND

The only way to create a workable budget is to adhere to this one simple rule:

Earn more than you spend.

Charles Dickens said "Annual income 20 pounds, annual expenditure 19 [pounds], 19 [shillings] and six [pence] result happiness. Annual income 20 pounds, annual expenditure 20 pounds ought and six, result misery." There's so much truth to that – you simply need to earn more than you spend.

Obviously, your goal is to earn **a whole lot more** than you spend, but if the numbers are close, that's okay; you can still work with that. Just don't lose track of the fact that you absolutely must earn more than you spend.

Later in this book we'll talk about both cutting costs and boosting income.

LET'S TAKE ACTION

1.   How much do I spend each month?

2.   What are my variable and non-essential expenses? What steps can I take to reduce these?

3.   What amount of income do I need to earn more than I spend? Do I have that income?

•   Use the budget planner on the next page as a guide to write down your income and expenses.

•   Using a 3-6-month history, if possible, come up with a monthly amount for variable and non-essential expenses.

•   Trim your variable and non-essential expenses until you reach an amount that fits comfortably within your income.

AFFIRMATION: I CREATE NEW HABITS TO HELP ME REACH MY GOALS

When I set a new goal, I try to think of anything I can do consistently, on a daily basis, to help me achieve it. Then I use mental cues, affirmations, and meditation to help me create that habit.

If the new goal is a positive character trait, like greater confidence, I strive to exhibit that attitude daily.

I create affirmations that remind me that I am a winner and I visualize conquering challenges with ease.

Soon enough, I realize that my habits have led me to my goal.

If I wish to become a philanthropist, I share my good fortune daily with those less fortunate, even if it is in very small amounts. The habit of automatically exhibiting this generosity catapults me to my goal.

If I wish to fund something like a new barn or a vacation, I get in the habit of automatically putting away bits of money daily, like dropping all my change into a jar or strictly paying cash for my purchases to avoid overspending. These thrifty strategies become habits in a short time that help me reach my goal.

I use this strategy for every goal I set. Every time I reinforce the habit, I strengthen it, which brings me closer to my goals!

My goal, today, is to create a new habit to help me maintain an optimistic attitude, no matter what. Every time I find myself with a negative thought, I can repeat a positive affirmation to replace it.

1. Do I rely on habits to give me an automatic push toward my goals?

2. What can I do consistently to help me achieve my latest goal?

3. What strategies can I use to help me reinforce those actions into a habit?

STAYING WITHIN YOUR BUDGET

Now that you've examined your income and expenses and created your budget, is it workable for you? The best budget is the one that works for you.

As you use it, feel free to adjust the amounts in the expense categories according to your realistic needs.

For example, if you had designated $300 per month for gas, but the gas prices rise, you may need to go back and raise the amount in the budget. That will mean carving the money out of some other section, though. And if there is no way to reasonably increase your gas budget, you need to find ways to decrease the expense.

Keep your budget up to date so you can continue to enjoy its benefits.

Does your budget have workable amounts, but you find that you're still having difficulty staying within your budget? Try the Envelope Method to easily keep track of your spending in each category.

THE ENVELOPE METHOD

The Envelope Method requires you to move to a cash-only system. Although this may sound like a challenge, it's really easier than you think!

This technique is an easy 3-step process:

Divide and conquer.

Each payday, cash your pay cheque at your bank, then divide the cash into different envelopes for each expense category.

For example, label one envelope Rent or Mortgage, one envelope Groceries, one envelope Car Payment, and continue in that manner until you have an envelope for every expense. Include an envelope for daily spending money for things like lunch or parking.

To determine how much to put into each envelope, look at your monthly budget and then divide the monthly expense by 2 if you get paid twice each month or 4 if you get paid every week. So if you get paid every week and your grocery bill is $400/month, take $100 out of each paycheck and put it into the Groceries envelope.

Use cash for your expenses. Once your pay cheque is divided up, it's very easy to keep track of your spending. That Groceries envelope, for example, is your grocery money for the week. Spend it wisely. Once you spend the money in that envelope, that's it for that week.

Effortlessly limit daily spending.

Each day, put the cash from that day's Spending Money envelope into your pocket or purse. That's your spending money for the day. When it's gone, stop spending!

Making a separate envelope for each day's spending money helps you stay within your budget without having to keep a mental figure of your balance in your mind at all times.

Besides making it easy to limit your spending to the budgeted amount, the Envelope Method also gives you a better sense of your money.

When you pay cash, you're more likely to see the real impact of your spending, even if it's small expenses. As you'll notice, small expenses really add up!

TIPS TO REDUCE YOUR EXPENSES

If you find that you're spending more than you make, you have two options:

- Make more money.

- Reduce the amount that you spend.

Honestly, can you think of ANY other way to manage it? You either need to reduce what you're spending, or you need to bring in more.

Juggling back and forth by moving credit card balances, begging for extensions, making minimum payments for the rest of your life – those aren't going to do anything good.

There are many techniques you can implement to bring in more money. These methods are discussed in a later module dedicated to increasing your income.

It's usually more difficult to reduce your fixed expenses, though it's not impossible. For example, if you rent an apartment and your lease is about to expire, perhaps you can find an apartment that costs less.

If your cable package has channels you don't use, ask about changing to a less expensive plan. Or ... and I know it sounds radical but ... consider that you may not need cable or even Netflix. In the same way, you may be able to reduce your cell phone plan.

Most likely, you'll make cuts in the variable expenses. Things like entertainment, food, gas, and even energy expenses can easily be reduced.

ENERGY SAVINGS

With energy, it's fairly simple to reduce your bill.

Turn lights off when you leave the room and switch to more energy efficient bulbs.

Last year we had an older house guest for a month, and she needed the house much brighter than we normally have it. I was worried about how it would look on our power bill, but because we have LED lights everywhere, the entire month costs us just $5 more. That doesn't mean you should always leave the lights on if you have efficient lights - $60/year is still $60.

Unplug your electronic devices when they aren't being used, because they use energy even when they're turned off if they're still plugged in.

If you have some money tucked away, newer models of appliances – like washers, dryers, and refrigerators – are also much more energy efficient and can pay for themselves in energy savings within a relatively short amount of time.

Other expense categories, like food and entertainment, have more options when it comes to saving money.

FOOD SAVINGS

Buying groceries is a necessary expense, but one that you have a lot of control over. A run to the grocery store can be devastating to your wallet if you let it, but it's also one of the best places to save money.

Here are some excellent ways to reduce the amount of money you spend at the grocery store:

Sales. Most grocery stores usually do a good job of putting everyday items on sale. If you buy the product on a regular basis, you might as well take advantage of the discounted price, and buy it when it's on sale.

The savings on each item may not be much, but you'll find that a few cents deducted here and there add up quite quickly.

Planning your weekly menu around what's on sale that week can turn into some significant savings.

Loyalty and Savings Card Programs. Plenty of grocery stores have implemented grocery card programs, which give you a wider range of discounts to take advantage of. For many of us, groceries are one of our biggest expenses, so the more ways we can save at the store, the better.

On rare occasions, they might even have a blanket discount, like 10% off the total bill, at certain times of the year. Watch for these promotions so you can make the best use of them.

Points earned on groceries can add up. Some people dislike them because it means the store is tracking your purchases. The reason they do that is to better stock shelves. Basically, they are paying you for market research, and it can be very profitable. With a family of six, I earn at least $600 in free groceries every year. Plus our grocery store has a gas station attached and the same program applies there.

Coupons. If you are in the United States, where coupons are common, they can be your most potent weapon against the grocery bill.

(Unfortunately they are far less common in other countries.)

You can find coupons in newspapers, flyers, and hundreds more online. These coupons can range from five cents to 100% off the cost of the item. You can't get better than free!

While a coupon for a certain product may limit you to one product per coupon, you can often pick up several of that item by simply using a coupon with each item. It's easy to obtain multiple coupons.

Some American stores even double the amount you see on the coupon, so you'll definitely want to look into which stores have such a program because it can add up to big savings very quickly.

Reducing your grocery bill by hundreds of dollars with coupons is surely a quick way to balance your budget while still eating like royalty!

Stockpiling. Buying in bulk has become a trend when it comes to grocery shopping. Stores like Sam's Club and Costco thrive on selling items in bulk at a low price. When used properly, buying in bulk can be a great way to save money. Paired with sales, and loyalty cards, I can buy a lot of food for great prices.

Be careful not to get carried away when shopping in stores that sell in bulk.

Twenty years ago, I remember calling Costco "the $400 store" because it often seemed like it was impossible to leave without spending $400. I haven't been there in years, but I imagine it's still just as easy to overspend. Keep in mind the space you have at home and watch expiration dates. Buying a case of pasta can be a great savings, while buying ten heads of romaine might not be.

One of the benefits of stockpiling is that you don't have to go to the grocery store as often.

Stores are designed to make you spend more than you intended to spend, so one of the best ways to spend less money is to stay out of the stores. Fewer trips to the grocery store saves you time, gas, and grocery money.

You can take advantage of buying in bulk even if you're single. Divide the cost and the spoils of your treasure trip with some friends. This way, all of you can save money and still avoid the inconveniences of stockpiling large amounts of stuff.

When you take advantage of these methods to save money on your regular expenses, it leaves room in your budget to increase your spending in other categories. In turn, staying within your budget becomes a whole lot easier!

LET'S TAKE ACTION!

1. How can I reduce the amount of energy I use?

2. Do my favorite stores offer deals, discounts or other savings? Are coupons an option that I can use?

3. Do I take advantage of the benefits of buying in bulk?

- Reduce your energy use as much as possible. Not only is this good for your wallet, but being eco-friendly helps all of us.

- Sign up for customer loyalty cards where you shop regularly.

- If coupons are an option, make use of them.

AFFIRMATION: I ENVISION MYSELF DEBT-FREE.

I envision myself debt-free, owing nothing to any man or institution. My books are in order and my accounts are balanced. I know that I can be free from debt because I am committed to my plan and I am responsible enough to make it happen.

I take pride in making sure that my family's financial future is safe. I am working toward leaving my children an inheritance of blessings, instead of financial ruin. The steps I am taking today will ensure that my family will be free from the burden of debt for generations to come.

The way I spend my money is a direct reflection of my priorities therefore I strive to invest in things of value and refrain from insignificant purchases.

When I want to buy something, I wait until I have saved enough money to make the purchase instead of buying on credit and acquiring more debt.

I have the ability to pay off all of my credit cards and loans by sending extra payments whenever I have surplus in my budget. When I pay off a debt, I stay away from new debt; instead I use the extra money for my savings and wealth building.

Temporarily, I have to make difficult cut backs in my spending in order to pay off my debt. I am simplifying my life and finding joy in things of true value. I refuse to accumulate more debt because I work hard for my money and deserve to be debt-free.

Today, I choose to be wise in my spending in order to be free from financial burdens. I see myself without debt; free to invest in my dreams. Free to give to others.

1.   What is my plan for becoming debt-free?

2.   Am I willing to make the necessary sacrifices to achieve my financial goals?

3.   How can I spend more wisely?

REDUCING EXPENSES WITHOUT AFFECTING YOUR LIFESTYLE

Entertainment, leisure activities, and lifestyle are often the first things to get cut when tightening the financial belt. It's unfortunate, but at the same time, this can save you quite a bit of money. Hobbies can be expensive, so it makes sense that this can be an effective way to reduce spending.

However, even though cutting yourself off entirely from your hobby (whether it be movies, books, comics, golf, or anything else) might be a good way to reduce spending, it is probably not a permanent reduction. As long as you are able to meet your necessary expenses, having some money in the budget for relaxing activities is actually healthy and much-needed!

There are ways you can reduce this expense without depriving yourself of the things you love. If you keep your wits about you, you can savor the joy of indulging yourself without the guilt of thinking about how it'll ruin your budget. There are quite a few ways to go about this.

CUSTOMER LOYALTY PROGRAMS

Similar to the grocery cards mentioned in chapter 2, these loyalty cards don't so much give you access to sale items (though they can often add an additional discount on sale items), rather they reward you with gift certificates or cards or free groceries for spending a certain amount of money. The standard rate is usually around $5 for every $100 spent, though it'll vary from store to store.

Some stores will have some sort of event where you can earn double or triple points. Even if they don't, the points don't usually expire, so you can work at your own rate to get to your desired number of points and your money-saving reward.

For example, some bookstores offer a rewards program as well as a blanket discount for their preferred customers. This works in your favor on two fronts and if you can find a bookstore that has such a setup, it's a great way to save money on things that you were going to buy anyway.

Some loyalty programs will offer a discount of perhaps 10% off the price. Depending on what state you live in, this won't do much more than negate the sales tax, but money is money and it can add up to significant savings.

So look for preferred customer programs in stores where you spend your "fun" money. These programs can help you continue to enjoy your hobby while spending less.

Please bear in mind, though, that nothing on sale is worthwhile if it puts you over your budget. If you need to pay down a large amount of debt in order to get your finances under control, even discounted luxuries will have to wait for a while.

BUYING USED

A great way to save money on your hobby is to buy used items. Many stores (including Walmart) have sections reserved for used games or movies.

Movie rental stores also sell used copies of movies and games. When compared to the price of a new item, there is usually a fairly drastic difference. Again, even the cost of $5 movies and games adds up, so do not buy them when you cannot pay your regular bills and keep your spending under control.

For the comic collector, many back issues can be found at a much lower price compared to the ticket price. There is also the option of trade paperbacks. Many comic readers have actually converted to that as it's often cheaper.

Book fanatics will also find that used bookstores are a boon when it comes to saving money on their literary addiction. Depending on the genre you enjoy and where you buy books, they can sometimes be found for a tenth or less of the original price. Banks and hospitals will often have shelves of donated books that can be bought for a dollar or two, and libraries sell off old books very inexpensively. I have found some real treasures that way.

ONLINE SHOPPING

Another way to save money is to buy things online. With popular websites like Amazon or eBay, you can often find the item you're looking for at a price much lower than the one you'll see in any store.

This also has the benefit of convenience as you don't have to go out to the store, saving you both time and gas money.

In addition to the low prices, Amazon will frequently offer items on sale. Most of the time, it's usually a couple of dollars (though discounts like that add up over time) but occasionally you can find expensive items for a drastically reduced price.

For example, recently Amazon marked down a bookshelf from $150 to $50. A trade paperback that was normally priced at $60 sold for a mere $10. Impulse shopping on the web can be a dangerous habit, but with markdowns like these and a healthy dose of willpower to stop while you're ahead, you can save a bundle.

RATION PURCHASES OVER TIME

There's nothing wrong with buying the things you want or indulging in a hobby once in a while.

It only becomes a budget issue when it causes you to spend more than you have coming in. I've always loved the quote from Erasmus "When I get a little money I buy books; and if any is left I buy food and clothes." We laugh (and maybe cringe if we can relate) because we know exactly what happens when someone puts a collection or hobby ahead of necessities.

If you're a collector and you feel the urge to go out and expand your library of whatever your pleasure may be, a way to meet your wallet halfway is to buy these items at a reduced rate.

So, if you're a movie fanatic, rather than going out and buying five or six new movies a week, reduce it to two or three every couple weeks, or rent the movies instead if that's a less expensive option.

If you enjoy going out on the town for entertainment, rather than going out every weekend, cut it down to perhaps once per month, and enjoy the company of family and friends at home on the other weekends. It could be your house or theirs. Vary it for a change of pace!

Maybe you have a gigantic Amazon wish list and you want to start putting a dent in that bad boy. Rather than whipping out your credit card and clicking compulsively until the card is maxed out, come up with a system where you pick items one by one.

Your system could be to allow one or two items each month, or you could decide to budget a specific amount, like $25 a month, for this one wish list. This technique has the added bonus of turning a variable expense into a constant one.

Even if you're a gadget junkie, you can still implement a similar system. Promise yourself that you won't go out and buy a high ticket gizmo until the one you just bought is paid off. This will keep you from getting buried in debt. It may take you longer to acquire the desired items, but you'll do it in a fiscally responsible way.

Implementing this kind of purchasing program is also beneficial in the long term. For instance, when you get a promotion or raise, training yourself to ration out the indulgences will allow you to keep more of your money and give you financial breathing room later on down the line.

LET'S TAKE ACTION

1. What indulgence do I spend the most money on?

2. What items do I feel comfortable buying used?

3. Do I need to be spending as much as I do on the items that I buy? How can I save on these purchases?

- Devise your own system to spread desired purchases out over time.

- Seek out used items for significant savings.

- Check for online discounts before buying in-store.

- Avoid buying another high end item until the previous one is completely paid off (and even then, make yourself wait just a little bit longer!)

AFFIRMATION: AS I ADJUST MY SPENDING HABITS, MY FINANCIAL SITUATION IMPROVES

My expectations for getting rid of debt and building wealth are reasonable. I know that it takes time to repair my finances and I am willing to invest that time in order to move beyond my debt.

Making sacrifices is a major part of improving my financial situation. I am willing to give up some of the things that I desire right now in order to afford a better future for my family.

When I shop, I bring a list with me in order to buy only the items that I need. I am free from the pressure to compete with others. I am grateful for what I have because my Creator has given me all that I need.

I have a plan for my financial future that involves me building sustainable wealth for my spouse and children. The passion I have for my financial goals helps me stay the course. When I am tempted to make an irresponsible purchase, I remind myself of my goals and exercise restraint.

My finances continually improve when I seek ways to cut unnecessary costs. I spend time each day reflecting on the driving force behind my purchases. I eliminate greed and competition from my heart by being grateful for what I have and giving to the less fortunate.

Today, I am improving my finances by refraining from unnecessary spending. I use my creativity to look for ways to save money knowing that the sacrifices I make today will be well worth it tomorrow.

Who can help me be accountable for my spending?

What do I want my financial situation to look like one year from today?

What is the driving force behind my purchases?

FRUGALITY MAY BE TERMED THE DAUGHTER OF PRUDENCE, THE SISTER OF TEMPERANCE, AND THE PARENT OF LIBERTY.

SAVING MONEY ON A DAY TO DAY BASIS

Everybody wants to save money, but few actually implement lasting solutions to help them save on a daily basis.

There are all sorts of savings plans that will suit long term as well as short term goals. Even on a daily basis, you can find ways to tuck money away for a rainy day.

Here are some easy strategies to help you get into a regular habit of saving money:

Create a separate spot for savings. Whether it's a sock drawer, an old wallet, or a separate bank account, one of the best ways to save money is to stash it somewhere and essentially forget about it. Use the concept of "out of sight, out of mind" to put the money aside. This is a method that I have often used because it just works.

It can be the leftover money from your paycheck, or a regular $10 a week, but if you make sure to put money aside consistently, you'll find that you can accrue a good chunk of change.

In this digital age we live in, you can set up systems like this automatically with your bank. With a few clicks of the mouse, you can have the bank transfer money from your checking to your savings account with no work needed on your part. Your bank can set up your transfers according to your preference, such as weekly, bi-weekly, or monthly.

If your income is small, your savings can be small, at least at first. When I first starting saving money, it was every loonie (our Canadian dollar coin) that passed through my hands. When I found that I was bringing ten of them to the bank each week, I started saving five dollar bills. Slowly increasing the amount that I automatically set aside made it fun and easy but still a challenge. Within the space of two years, with an income that was below Canada's Low Income Cut Off, we had saved enough for a sizable down payment on a property.

Remember that small deposits can add up quickly. Do you feel that saving money means you need to set aside huge chunks of dough in order to be worth the effort? The truth is quite the opposite! Even if you can only put aside a couple of dollars here and there, that will add up later on down the line. Especially if you have debt, remember that every single dollar you pay down is worth a lot more than a dollar. A penny saved may be a penny earned, but a penny put on your debt is more like a dime. Pay off your debt before you begin saving.

By using an interest-bearing savings account, you'll allow the interest to add to the savings. As the account grows, so too will the amount you receive in interest. This means that the longer you save, the easier it'll become. It may take a while, but once you get the ball rolling, the effect will snowball and allow the numbers to really climb. It pays to take the time to find a bank that still has interest-bearing savings accounts.

Find bargains wherever possible. One of the best ways to save money is to keep your eyes open for money-saving opportunities and take advantage of them. For example, many of your day to day expenses can be reduced simply by changing your routine.

Finding a more efficient solution can be a great way to keep more money in your pocket. If, for example, you enjoy having a soda while you're at work, rather than going to the vending machine and spending a dollar (or more) on a bottle, buy a 24 pack and bring it with you in a cooler. It's much cheaper and it can save you a substantial amount every week.

A good quality insulated coffee mug (and a vacuum bottle if you need more than a single serving) means that you can make coffee at home. Thermos has always made the best vacuum bottles and now they make travel mugs that will keep your coffee hot for twelve hours outside on a cold day!

You can use the same strategy for lunch. The best way to save money on lunch is to bring one from home. You'll find that the amount you spend on two or three restaurant meals could provide you with two or three weeks of meals from home. Save the eating out for when it's important to you.

Even when money is tight, you can still enjoy seeing your savings grow when you combine automatic withdrawals with simple daily saving strategies. For example, you can put the money you save from changing a few routines into an interest-bearing savings account.

LET'S TAKE ACTION

1.   How much money do I have left over after a pay period?

2.   Do I have a place where I can stash the extra cash?

3.   What can I do to cut my spending and save more?

- Decide on a safe place to "stash away" money, as this will help to keep it "out of sight, out of mind".

- Save money by bringing lunch from home or buying your favorite snacks from the grocery store instead of using the vending machine.

- Have the bank automatically withdraw money into a savings account for you

AFFIRMATION: EXERCISING RESTRAINT IN MY FINANCES ALLOWS ME TO BUILD WEALTH

I envision myself with a savings account large enough to secure my family in the face of change. I am proactive toward giving the gift of financial security to my family and myself.

My goal is to be able to retire and continue to live well. In order to reach that goal, I must make some adjustments to my current lifestyle. By living below my means, I am setting myself up for a lifetime of provision.

My spending habits are a reflection of my true desires. I research before making major purchases. Comparison-shopping helps me to get the best deals available.

My motivation for making purchases is need, not greed. Before I buy, I ask myself, "Do I really need this right now?" The money I am saving by exercising restraint is going toward more important things in life, such as college funds or retirement savings.

I am free from the pressure of trying to impress others, because I am loved for who I am, not for what I have.

If I am out with my friends and one makes an expensive purchase, I am fine just sitting back and watching, without needing to make a large purchase of my own.

In the future, I will appreciate my wise financial decisions. I am building wealth to secure myself and leave an inheritance for my children.

When I focus on the good things that I have, I overflow with enough gratitude to drown out the materialistic side of me. The self-control needed to abstain from unnecessary purchases is within me.

Today, I count my blessings and appreciate what I have. I envision myself enjoying my future thanks to the decisions I make today.

1.   What can I do to resist the temptation to spend too much?

2.   When was the last time I balanced my budget and made a financial plan?

3.   What is my vision for my financial future?

SHORT TERM SAVINGS

Saving isn't only for the distant future. While that's all well and good, sometimes you'll want to save for a more immediate purpose. Maybe you want to take a family vacation or buy a new computer. Perhaps it's a very large expense like the down payment on a new home.

Whatever the case may be, purchases like this require some saving up ahead of time.

SAVING STRATEGIES FOR SHORT TERM GOALS

These techniques can help you effectively reach your intended goal:

Plan ahead. The more prepared you are, the better. If you're planning a major event for your 20th anniversary, for example, you could start saving for it just after your 19th passes by. If you're looking to buy a new house and you need a down payment, look at the amount you need and determine how long it would take you to reasonably acquire that amount of money.

All you need to do is find the price of the item, decide when you want to make the purchase, and then divide the price by the number of weeks until the purchase date. The answer tells you how much to put aside each week.

Start planning for your special purchase well ahead of the event because the longer time you have to save, the less money you'll need to save during each pay period.

The power of the change jar

Did you have a piggy bank (or some variation of it) when you were a child? Piggy banks instill the idea of saving money in you at a young age. Little did you know that the same principle could be applied later on in life! Your extra change can be a very powerful savings tool.

At the end of each day, simply put your left-over change into a container and leave it there. It's rather brilliant in its simplicity. You usually round-up when you pay anyway, so as far as you're concerned, that money doesn't exist. Take advantage of the fact that you round up the amount in your mind.

As time goes on, the container will fill up and that jar of change will turn out to be a pretty hefty chunk of money.

Roll up your coins and take them to the bank to trade them in. It may not be as convenient as those coin counting machines in the grocery store, but you'll save the 8% fee. Besides, you can make a game out of it with your kids!

This is a method that my godfather always used. He was a wealthy businessman from the Netherlands and he always told my father "Take care of the pennies – the dollars are big enough to take care of themselves." Every night he emptied his pockets into a large jar and when it was full, he took it to the bank.

Put off superfluous purchases

If you're saving up for a major purchase, a good way to speed up the process is to cut out any unnecessary purchases. Yes, you can live without that novel that was just released and you can probably pass on that beautiful little goat at the livestock auction. (Why are you at the livestock auction if you're trying to save money? That's as bad as hanging out in the second hand book store!) You can always pick up the item after you get what you were saving for. Putting off unimportant purchases will make it easier for you to reach your goal – and your reward – that much sooner.

The electronic change jar

A lot of banks have implemented automatic transfer programs that mirror the change jar. It started with Bank of America's "Keep the Change" program, where any debit purchase triggered a transfer of the difference up to the next dollar. For example, a $5.85 purchase would transfer $0.15 to your savings account. It's worthwhile to see if your bank has a program like this.

Like the change jar, it's a great way to subtly put money aside. One of the great perks is that some banks match a small percentage and add it as a deposit to your savings account at the end of the year. It's like getting free money just for saving your change!

Using these short term saving tips will allow you to truly savor your end goal knowing that you paid for it in full. Imagine the pride you'll feel when you pay for your next vacation with the money you've already saved, instead of maxing out your credit cards. Then, it's even sweeter when you aren't deluged with bills when you get home!

Rather than spending the next year paying for last year's vacation (plus interest), you can get something else you want! And you can do it all by growing your savings in ways that don't make you deprive yourself.

LET'S TAKE ACTION

1. What do I want to save up for and how much does it cost?

2. In what time frame would I like to buy this item?

3. What am I willing to do to save without feeling deprived and resentful?

- Find a jar or container to store your extra change.

- Delay unimportant purchases until you reach your goal to speed up reaching your reward.

- Put aside a set amount of money from each pay to contribute to your goal.

LONG TERM SAVINGS

Along with saving for your short-term goals and tucking some money aside for a rainy day, it's also important to implement long term savings.

Long term savings are typically used for funding your retirement or your children's college expenses. Establishing a plan for long term savings can seem like a daunting task at first, but it's one that you can accomplish if you put your mind to it. The great news is that, with long term savings, you can benefit drastically from the interest build-up.

Just as with short term saving, there are important things to consider in your long term savings plans. For example, the longer you have for saving up, the less money you need to allocate each month toward your goal.

THE POWER OF COMPOUND INTEREST

Let's look at an example of the effect of interest over the long term. If you start a retirement plan when you're 25, and put in $100 per month for 40 years, here are your results at an 8% interest rate:

Total amount saved: $353,855.46

Total Principle: $48,000 ($100/month for 40 years)

Total Interest Earned: $305,855.46

Compare the two figures above. It shows show you the power of compound interest. Over $305,000 of your savings is from interest alone! As your savings grow, you're getting paid interest on the interest you already received.

So it's in your best interest to take advantage of all the interest you can and start as early as possible on your long term savings.

SAVING FOR COLLEGE

With the price of tuition skyrocketing at unimaginable rates, it's very important that you have a plan to prepare for these costs.

Here are some strategies that can help you build a hefty college fund:

Start early. It's best to start a college fund in your child's first year, as that will give you as much time as possible to save the necessary funds. You can set up an account in their name, set up a savings bond, or simply open an account in your name and allocate it as a college fund.

Assemble a team. Try to get other relatives involved. Most aunts, uncles, and grandparents are happy to contribute to a child's education. It doesn't need to be a drastic amount, but every little bit helps.

Instill a good savings mentality in your child and let him put his little piece into the pie. Regular contributions from your child, even if it's only a dollar, teach him the importance of saving, and this value will benefit him the rest of his life! It also increases the college fund. When he's ready to use it, he'll feel pride in knowing that he helped build it.

Seek security plus a higher interest rate. Browse around and find which bank has the highest interest rate. Online banks tend to have higher interest rates for savings accounts, but do your research and see which one pays the best rates.

As you deposit more money and the balance grows, so too will the amount that the bank will pay you in interest. A difference of even 1% can have a big effect on your total savings.

Many investment products pay more interest than a savings account at your bank. Look into using mutual funds, exchange-traded funds, and other investments to increase your rate of return. However, as the interest rate grows, so does the risk. A college fund may not span enough years to tolerate much risk.

So keep safety in mind as you search for higher returns.

In Canada, the federal government will match Registered Education Savings Plan contributions, so take advantage of that.

STUDENT LOANS AND GOVERNMENT AID

Even with savings in a college fund, there's a good chance that you or your child will need to take out some form of student loan to help pay the bill, especially if they attend a school far from home or pursue post-graduate degrees.

You can apply for a loan through your local bank, but the federal government also offers financial aid should you need it. Federal student loans generally charge lower interest, so it may save you some money to look into it.

In addition, unlike most loans, federal student loans don't activate immediately. Depending on the terms of the loan, you can usually delay the start of payments until after your child graduates. This allows the student to focus on his or her schoolwork. After that, there's often a "grace period" of a few months before the bills start rolling in.

SCHOLARSHIPS

One of the best ways a student can save money on college is to get a scholarship. These can be offered on an academic or athletic basis. Some offer a completely paid-for education, while others cover only a portion of the fees. Of course, some is better than none. With the cost of education as high as it is, any assistance is beneficial.

A major benefit of scholarships, of course, is that you don't have to pay them back!

When you do your research, you'll discover that there are tons of scholarships available! If you'd like more information, visit your local bookstore or do some research on the internet.

Also, once your child has decided on a college, take advantage of the college's financial aid office. This office gives you access to a multitude of scholarships available from the college's alumni association, as well as a host of other sources.

SAVING FOR RETIREMENT

Retirement is the big kahuna when it comes to savings goals and it's also the most important! The better you plan, the sooner you can reach your goals and retire free from financial stress.

While basic savings accounts may suit your needs for the most part, it's recommended that you look into other investment services that can provide a better rate of return on your funds. In the United States, there are 2 basic retirement accounts that are the preferred method for most working people, the 401(k) and the Individual Retirement Account (IRA).

IRA'S (USA)

IRA's are retirement accounts that you can open with your bank. They allow you to create a portfolio of stocks, bonds, and mutual funds that will provide a much greater return than that of a simple savings account. There are two general types of IRA's.

TRADITIONAL (USA)

The traditional IRA is the actual investment account. You can fund it with cash or cash equivalents, so while baseball cards and comic books can make great investments, you can't fund an IRA with one.

One of the perks of the IRA is that the money you deposit isn't taxed. Basically, when you siphon off some money into that account it's considered "pretax" dollars. This allows you to legally keep some of your money away from Uncle Sam, at least for a while.

When you hit retirement and start taking the money out, that's when they tax it and consider it your income. However, at that point you will be probably withdrawing much less than you are currently making.

If you're going to deposit money into a traditional IRA, ensure that you don't need that money at all. Taking money out of an IRA before you hit age 70 will incur penalties, plus you'll have to pay income taxes on it as well.

ROTH IRA'S (USA)

Roth IRA's are different from the traditional in that these aren't tax deductible. While the deposits are considered "after tax" dollars, it's much easier to get to your money if you need it with far fewer penalties involved.

There's a deposit limit of $5,000 per year into your Roth IRA account ($6,000 if you're over age 50). If you have both a Roth and Traditional IRA, than that number applies to both accounts combined. The limit is still $5,000 or $6,000; it doesn't double just because you have two accounts.

401(K) (USA)

Another option you have when it comes to retirement is the 401(k). Unlike IRA's, where you sign up through your bank, a 401(k) is done through your employer. 401(k) accounts have an annual deposit limit of $16,500.

Much like an IRA, any contribution will not be taxed until you withdraw from it. Earnings made from the 401(k) are also tax deferred until the money is withdrawn. Also like an IRA, taking money out of your 401(k) before you reach the minimum age (60 in this case) will result in hefty fees and penalties.

One of the major perks of a 401(k) is that some employers match your deposits up to a certain percent. This will essentially put free money into your account and expand your nest egg quite significantly.

TFSA AND RRSP (CANADA)

In Canada, you can get what's called a Tax Free Savings Account (TFSA). You must be 18 in order to open a TFSA. You can withdraw money at any time without tax penalties. While the deposits aren't tax deductible, money made from that account isn't taxed.

Canadians also have what is called a Registered Retirement Savings Plan (RRSP). This is much closer to America's Traditional IRA, only the deposit limit's much higher than that of America's. It also doubles as a 401(k) as employers can put money from your paycheck straight into the account.

INDIVIDUAL SAVINGS ACCOUNT IN THE UNITED KINGDOM

In the UK, you can get what is referred to as an Individual Savings Account. The ISA can be divided into two components: a cash component and then a stocks and shares component. It's possible to transfer funds from the cash to the stocks component, but not the other way around.

LET'S TAKE ACTION

1.   What financial goal is necessary for me to retire comfortably?

2.   Does my employer match my retirement fund contributions?

3.   What type of retirement fund best suits my needs?

•   Start saving NOW to allow earnings to compound and accumulate.

•   If your employer matches your contributions, do your best to add the maximum amount you can so that you get the best return possible.

•   Be aware of penalties for early withdrawal – leave the money alone

AFFIRMATION: I AM MORE THAN CAPABLE OF GREAT SUCCESS.

My abilities and talents render me more than qualified to achieve my dreams. The quality of my skills and the strength of my will power exceed the challenges ahead of me. When I focus on my strengths instead of my weaknesses, I achieve greater success.

I can propel myself high above any hurdle that stands in my way. Determination is the wind beneath my wings as I rise above obstacles. Preparation is what helps me overcome the fear of taking risks.

I seek knowledge and educate myself continuously in order to be confident in my abilities. I feel comfortable asking questions so I may learn from those I admire. My eyes are trained to spot and retain useful information. I seize every opportunity that I can to expand my capabilities.

I present myself with credibility. Others look forward to working with me because they are confident in my ability to succeed. I have earned the respect of those around me by upholding a high standard for myself. I am fortunate to have a team of people that I can count on to support me in my endeavors.

Success surrounds me like a shield. Great success is within my reach. When I accept my value, I free myself to achieve my potential. My work is marked by passion and integrity. I am more than capable of great success because I work hard for my dreams.

I am well grounded. I am fully capable of managing the responsibilities that come with great success. With my abilities in one hand and a strong support group in the other, I am able to be successful beyond my wildest expectations.

Today, I am confident that success is within my reach.

1. How can I better prepare myself for success?

2. Have I set high standards for myself?

3. What can I do to increase my knowledge and skills?

USING YOUR CREDIT CARDS WISELY

Credit cards are convenient on so many levels. With credit cards, you don't have to carry large amounts of cash, you can pay quickly and easily, and you don't even have to pay immediately. While the benefits are numerous, credit cards also carry a serious responsibility.

It's very tempting to go on spending sprees or neglect to pay your bill on time, but irresponsible use of a credit card can lead to severe financial repercussions, including mounting debt, wasted dollars, harassment from bill collectors, lowering your credit score, and even bankruptcy!

Fortunately, credit cards aren't a terribly complicated concept. A good dose of common sense and fiscal responsibility will go a long way.

SIMPLE CREDIT CARD MANAGEMENT TIPS

Follow these tips to manage your credit cards wisely:

Start with debit cards. Almost all checking accounts now come with a debit card. If you're considering getting a credit card, it would be smart to start with a debit card as training.

A debit card operates in a similar capacity to a credit card: the merchant runs it through the scanner and you sign the receipt. The only difference is that, where credit cards put off the payment, debit cards process the transaction immediately. This restricts your spending to only what you have in your bank account.

Only buy what you can afford. A good rule to follow when it comes to credit card use is to simply ask yourself if you have the money for your purchase. If you don't, then don't buy it.

If you have a payday coming between the purchase and the arrival of the monthly credit card bill, you can usually flirt with the line, but when it comes to credit, it's usually better to err on the side of caution, especially if you're new to the world of credit cards.

Wait to buy high end items. There are rare occasions where it's not feasible to wait, like if you need immediate car repairs. However, most expensive items can wait until you save the funds to buy it.

Money Mastery: Creating a Life Without Debt

If you do buy an expensive item, quit using the card until it's paid off in full. A major challenge you may face with credit cards is that you'll buy some large indulgence, and then you'll continue to use the card. Doing so makes the balance out of reach and nearly impossible to pay back at the high credit card interest rates.

If you stop using the card until the item is paid off in full, the interest charges will be kept to a minimum and you won't find yourself drowning in debt.

Small purchases add up. Even more dangerous than the big purchases are the little ones. It seems paradoxical, but it's true. With a large purchase, you (ideally) go in knowing that this is a big deal and compensate accordingly. It's trickier with smaller, but regular purchases, like lunch or a tank of gas.

We tend to dismiss small charges as insignificant: five bucks here and there.

Before we realize it, though, we've racked up a hefty balance!

Keep track of your purchases. A good way to ensure your purchases don't spiral out of control is to keep track of all of your purchases. A spreadsheet or even a small notebook should meet your needs quite well.

Pay off the card in full whenever possible. Ideally, when your credit card bill comes in, you'll be able to pay off the balance in full. If it's possible to do so, then do it. If you can't pay it off right away, then pay it as quickly as you can.

Paying your credit card in full keeps you out of debt, saves you a ton of money on interest and fees, and helps raise your credit score.

Credit cards are convenient and can help you to maintain an excellent credit score, when used appropriately. They grant you power, and like any power, it requires an equal amount of responsibility. (Remember – Spiderman taught us that!)

LET'S TAKE ACTION

1. Before making a purchase, I ask myself: Do I NEED to buy this now, or can it wait until later? If I do buy this, how long will it take me to pay it off?

2. How many times do I use my credit card every month? Do I have the money to pay it off before the due date?

*   Start with (or return to) a debit card. It is an excellent training tool to learn how to handle the temptation of credit cards.

*   Watch the small purchases. They can sneak up on you!

*   Have some way to keep track of your transactions, whether it's an app, a computer software or a notepad and pencil. Don't rely on memory.

*   If you make large purchases, cut yourself off from the card until you've paid it in full.

AFFIRMATION: CHIPPING AWAY AT A BIG TASK KEEPS ME FOCUSED AND QUICKLY BUILDS MOMENTUM

When I have a large project to complete, or a big goal to achieve, I divide it into a series of small tasks. Each task is easily accomplished, so I can dive right in. Completing these mini goals keeps me going and drives me forward to success.

This method sets me up for success every time. Once I make my plan and get started, I know without a doubt that I can succeed. I can keep my focus throughout the project, moving easily from one small task onto the next.

Often, the hardest part of any big project is getting started. The end can seem so far away when I'm looking at the project from the outset! So I schedule the quickest, easiest tasks for the beginning. This allows me to get started without delay.

As I complete more and more of these small tasks, I feel the force of my momentum pushing me forward to the next ones. This energy even helps me overcome obstacles in my path so I can continue the project until it is complete!

It's like chopping down a tree. No matter how large the tree may be, I know I can cut it down by chipping away at it bit by bit. My small tasks are like the little chips of the tree. Each little chip only requires a small action, yet they all add up to success.

Today, my plan is to follow this strategy for all my projects so I can chip my way to success!

1.   Am I procrastinating on starting a large project right now?

2.   How can I divide my next project into easily achievable tasks?

3.   What's the easiest task I can put at the beginning so I can get started right away?

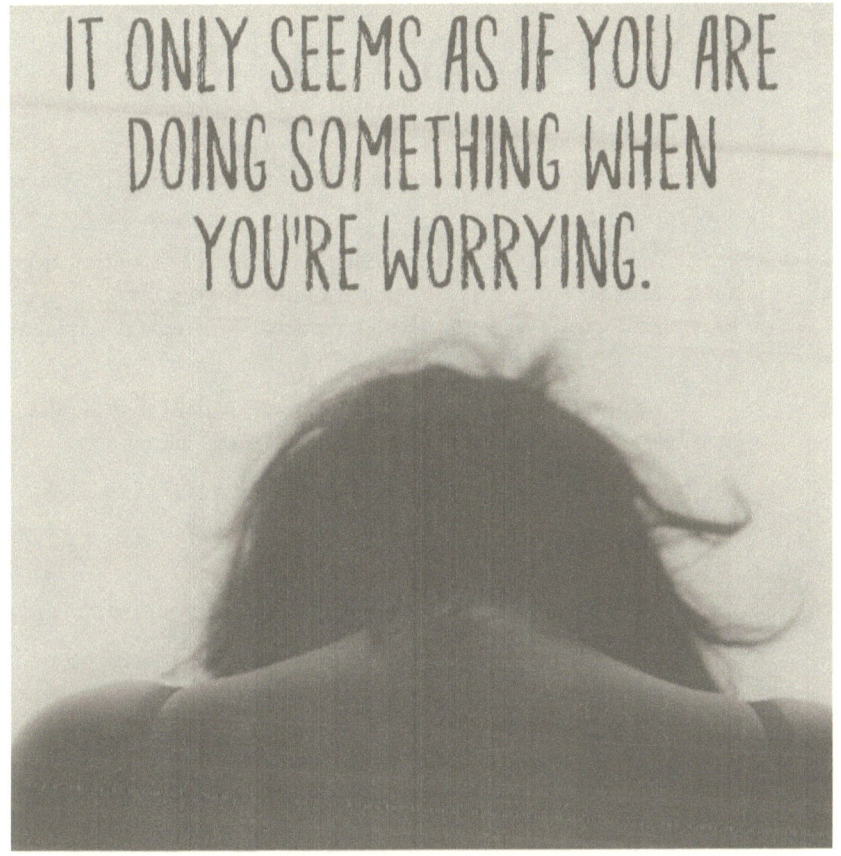

GETTING OUT OF DEBT

While we all would ideally pay off our credit cards in full every month, that doesn't always happen. Plus, modern life often forces us into debt.

If you want to go to college, buy a car, or own a home, you'll most likely take out loans to pay for these things. Even if you do keep your credit card usage in check, it's difficult to remain completely debt-free.

But fear not! While your mountain of debt may be daunting, it's possible to get to the top and clear your financial name!

First, let's tackle your credit card balances.

CREDIT CARD DEBT

Try these tactics to reduce and eliminate your credit card debt:

Pay off more than you use. The only way to gain ground on your credit card balance is to pay off more than you use. If you make the minimum payment of $20 and then spend $50, you're not going to be getting out of debt anytime soon. Also, be sure to take into account the interest charge as well as other fees when calculating each month's total expenditure.

Pay off small balances first. If you have a card with a balance of only a couple of hundred dollars, paying that one off first will quickly eliminate one bill altogether, allowing you to reroute the money that would've gone towards paying that bill to one of the higher interest cards.

This also eliminates the hassle of interest charges on that card. With no balance on the card, you'll be saving yourself in the long term as well.

Make high interest cards the priority. While the above rule is helpful in a handful of situations, by and large you'll want to target the higher interest cards first and knock them out of the way.

Once a balance is paid off, use the money for that payment to pay off other balances. Knocking a credit card balance out is a major relief! It's one less payment you have to worry about and one less monkey on your back. Use this success as momentum to take care of the other bills.

Follow this strategy:

Determine the amount you need to pay on each of your cards – minimum payments on all of them, plus an amount that will quickly pay off your smallest, highest-interest card quickly. Let's say, for example, that you are making total payments of $400, with $50 each on four cards and $200 on the card that you're paying off quickly.

Pay off credit card #1 with $200 payments.

Add these funds to your payment for credit card #2. This is very important. Don't let anything divert these funds somewhere else. You are now paying $50 each on three cards and $250 on card #2.

Pay this amount on credit card #2 every month until it's paid off.

Once those two cards are paid off: Add the funds from credit cards #1 and

#2 to pay card #3. At this point, you are now paying $300 per month on card #3.

Pay this amount on credit card #3 every month until it's paid off.

Next: Add in the payments from cards #1, #2, and #3 toward card #4.

Continue this strategy until you've eliminated your credit card debt.

There is nothing special about my choice of $400. What you want initially is to determine how much you can put towards debt repayment and the minimum amount that must be paid on all the cards. Choose the card with the highest interest rate and lowest balance and make it your card #1.

This will greatly speed up the overall process of getting your cards paid off and wiping the slate clean.

What's really amazing is that, once you've paid off your first card, you'll be able to use this strategy without paying more for your monthly bills than you were in the first place. Yet, the momentum gets bigger and bigger for eliminating that debt, like a snowball rolling down a hill.

Avoid skipping payments. If you do miss a payment, they'll add the missed payment to the next month's bill in addition to the interest, late fees, and maybe even over-limit fees. This could even cause your annual interest rate to increase. Once this starts, it's difficult to get out of the pattern. The charges add up quick and your balance will skyrocket.

Not only will this affect your balance, but the credit card company will also call you. Avoiding the call only makes things worse.

You would think that they would get the point, but they don't. They call, and call, and call, and call. It's incredibly annoying and you're better off doing whatever you can to avoid missing the scheduled payment.

Debt consolidation can be your friend. Many times, it benefits you to consolidate several of your debts into just one balance from one creditor. Not only can you take advantage of a better interest rate, but you also eliminate several of your monthly bills. Often, the one payment on the consolidated balance is less than the total of your previous bills.

If you can get a loan from the bank, it can help you out. Using that money to pay off your credit cards will reduce your overall interest charges. When going this route, avoid using your credit cards again after paying them off. That defeats the purpose entirely and will result in your debt becoming worse than it was before you started.

Many credit cards offer a lower interest rate for the first year on a new card, and they invite you to transfer your balances from your higher interest cards to your new one. On these offers, be sure to read the fine print. Many things, including one late payment, can void the initial offer and result in an increased interest rate even higher than you had on your old cards.

Consolidating your debts can free up money that you can use to pay down your remaining balances. It's one more way you can get out of debt without using any more money than before you started.

Use windfalls to pay down your credit card debt. If you come across some extra cash, use the money to pay off as many of those balances as you can. In essence, your windfall is multiplied when you think of all the money in interest charges it will save you.

Plus, the faster you become debt-free, the faster you can use your money for whatever you want rather than just sending it all to your creditors!

Eliminating your credit card debt can bring you immense relief and greatly enhance your financial future. But what about other types of debt? Luckily, there are some effective methods you can use to save money and pay off these debts in record time!

TAX DEPARTMENT

If you owe money to the tax department (IRS in the United States, CRA in Canada), make paying them off your highest priority!

With their many fees and interest charges, a debt to the tax department costs you even more than credit cards, including possibly your home, business, and any money you have in your bank accounts.

Yes, they can even go in and grab whatever is sitting in your bank account at any time! They can take your home or business and sell them to get the money you owe them. This is true even if your home is worth many times what you owe them.

Borrowing the money from a bank or charging what you owe to your credit cards is infinitely more beneficial than extending the time you take to pay whatever you owe to the tax department. Even refinancing your mortgage to get the cash needed to pay them can be an option you may wish to consider.

Whatever you do, don't mess with your country's tax department! Pay them off immediately with whatever resources you can gather.

STUDENT LOANS

In many cases, your student loans have a lower interest rate than your other debts, so they may not be as high in priority when it comes to paying off your debt. Also, you can often stretch out the payment period over many years so the payments aren't a burden.

However, these payments tend to add up because there can be multiple loans for every year of college. Plus, the total balance can be astronomical simply due to the high cost of attending college.

Check into consolidating these loans to eliminate multiple payments every month. Contact your lender(s) and see what programs they have for combining the loans. You may be able to continue receiving a low interest rate while only having to make one payment that's less than the total of your multiple payments.

While consolidating can give you a handle on managing these loans, at some point, you'll want to finish paying these off also. Once you've eliminated your credit card debt, you may want to apply the extra funds towards this debt to get this monkey off your back as well.

CAR LOANS AND OTHER SHORT-TERM BANK LOANS

These types of loans also usually carry lower interest rates than your credit cards. Depending on how long it takes you to pay off your credit cards, which are a higher priority, you may find that these loans reach their term and disappear while you're paying off your other debt.

In order to prevent car payments that never end, consider saving up the money in advance and paying cash for your next car. A used car, even if it only has 100 miles on it, costs thousands less than a new one and the original warranty is still in effect, just as if you had bought it new. Shop around for your best deal, both locally and on the internet.

MORTGAGE LOANS

You can save tens of thousands of dollars in interest on your mortgage loan and pay it off 10 - 15 years sooner simply by restructuring your loan to an accelerated bi-weekly plan, instead of a monthly one. With a bi-weekly plan, you pay half of a regular loan payment every 2 weeks, instead of a whole loan payment once each month.

The secret is that, when you pay half a normal payment every two weeks, you end up making 26 payments in a year. This adds up to 13 regular monthly loan payments, instead of the 12 you would make on the monthly plan.

In order to set up your loan this way, you need to arrange it with your lender. It does no good whatsoever to just send in half of your regular loan payment. If you try this, the lender will either return it to you for sending in the wrong amount, or simply sit on it (with no benefit to you) until the other half of the payment comes in.

This method is especially easy for you to implement if you get paid on a weekly or bi-weekly basis. So make that call to your lender. The sooner you start, the more you save!

If you're getting a new mortgage loan or refinancing your mortgage, have them set up your loan this way in the first place. You'll be absolutely astounded at the difference.

Alternatively, you can send in an extra monthly payment each year and have the lender apply it to the principal. The total amount you save may be less than with the bi-weekly structure, but it'll still reduce the mortgage by years – and thousands of dollars – by paying it off sooner. The trick in this method is maintaining the discipline to send in that extra monthly payment every year.

YOU CAN DO IT!

Paying off your debt can be difficult, but it's very possible when you use these techniques. Not only do these methods make it possible for you to be debtfree, but they can also save you many thousands of dollars in interest charges, making your debt-free celebration date arrive years sooner!

When the going gets rough, just keep your eyes on your prize. Imagine what it'll be like to be debt-free. When you get your paychecks, all that money will be yours to spend as you please! No more mailboxes filled with bills for debt payments! No more harassing calls from creditors!

Those debts aren't the boss of you, so take control of your debt today and enjoy the freedom that a debt-free life can bring.

LET'S TAKE ACTION

1. Which credit card or loan payment is costing me the most in interest fees?

2. Can I pay off some of these loans without a penalty? If there is a penalty, is it financially better to take the penalty or pay the interest?

3. How much am I spending on interest each month?

4. How can I cut expenses to speed up my debt repayment?

5. Can I move some of my balances to a lower interest loan?

    •   Make a written plan for paying off your debt and stick to your plan.

    •   Consolidate as much of your debt as possible. This will reduce the number of bills you have to pay each month, which is less psychologically daunting.

    •   Pay off the high interest balances first in order to get out of debt as quickly as possible.

    •   When one debt is paid, immediately reroute that money toward the next debt in your list in order to compound the effect.

AFFIRMATION: MY DEBT DOES NOT CONTROL ME. I AM IN CONTROL OF MY DEBT.

I maintain effective financial habits that make saving money automatic and keep me from sinking into debt. As a result, I effortlessly move toward financial freedom and a debt-free lifestyle.

Every time I get paid, a portion of my income automatically goes into savings. I figure that if I don't see it I won't miss it!

I make a detailed budget, including both necessary expenses and fun money and I stick to it.

I trust myself to use credit cards appropriately. I am sure to stay within my budget so that each month I can pay off whatever I charge. This strategy builds great credit, too!

If something costs more than the monthly budget allows, I save up for it. I only use extended credit for the big things, like a car or a house, and I get great interest rates on the big items because of my wise financial habits.

I also do little things each day that add up to a lot of money over time. At the end of each day, I put all my change into a jar and start fresh with only bills the next day. I plan my meals so I can prepare food at home rather than having to pick up fast food due to a hectic schedule. I make my own coffee rather than pick some up on the way to work.

Today, I am planning a nice vacation, paid for with cash, because my great financial habits free up the funds for me to enjoy such rewards.

- Am I effortlessly moving toward financial freedom?

- Have I taken the trouble to make a flexible budget that I can stick to?

- What habits can I start that will put me more in control of my debt?

WAYS TO BRING IN EXTRA CASH

Working the standard 9-5 job may get the bills paid, but it rarely provides the financial cushion that we wish it did. Luckily, there are ways to boost your income.

BOOSTING YOUR INCOME

Ask for a raise. Sometimes the simplest solution is the best one. If you have a good record and show that you're willing to work hard, most bosses will consider the idea of giving you a raise. Rather than make things more complicated than they need be, why not start with your primary source of income and see if they can throw a few extra bucks your way?

Find a bank with better interest rates. This won't provide immediate relief, but it will add a little to your balance every month. If you're saving for the long haul, this can have quite an impact. Online banks like ING Direct tend to have higher interest rates than those of the "brick and mortar" companies.

If you decide to look for an online bank, be sure to make sure it's FDIC insured so you know that your money is secure and that the bank is reputable.

If you're happy with your bank, look at other types of accounts. Money market accounts often offer higher interest rates than savings accounts while also allowing you to write checks. While there's a limit on the number of checks you can write, it's still pretty convenient to have the best of both worlds in one account.

Get a second job. Although exhausting, getting an additional job may enable you to pull in enough extra income each month to make ends meet. It doesn't have to be a glamorous job, and even a part time gig can help you get back on your feet.

Unless you really enjoy your second job, this is a tip that's only to be used temporarily for an extra income boost. Working yourself that much is ripe to burn you out and there are other things in life to enjoy besides making money.

Offer your services. A good way to pick up some extra income is to offer your services to others. Offer to babysit your neighbor's kids so they can go out, set up a lawn-mowing service in the summer, shovel snow in the winter, paint houses, and more. Some of these services may help you pick up a few hundred dollars extra every weekend.

Buy things at garage sales and sell them at flea markets. This can turn into a lucrative weekend pastime. You can find some real bargains at garage sales that provide great profits when you resell them.

USING THE INTERNET TO YOUR ADVANTAGE

The dawn of the digital age has changed the way business works forever. Not only has it changed the way companies distribute goods, but it has also given people the power to go into business for themselves and advertise their services to a world-wide audience. If you're looking to make a little cash on the side, you have a variety of options at your disposal.

Sales. With sites like eBay and Amazon, you can now put money in your pocket by selling things you no longer need. Have an old television, DVD, or Atari 2600 that you want to get rid of? Someone on the web will gladly buy it. Sell all your unused stuff and clean out your clutter while making money.

If you liked the idea about picking up items at garage sales and reselling them for a profit, you can also use eBay as another place to sell your garage sale purchases.

Writing. The internet has given self publishers an excellent venue to showcase their work. You can easily write "how-to" books (even short ones) and sell them through Amazon or Clickbank.com. Amazon has a program called CreateSpace.com where you only need to upload the digital version of your book and they print and mail them out as they're ordered. This means no inventory since the books are printed on-demand.

If you're a stay at home parent, this is a perfect choice. You get to work your own hours, write about topics that excite you, and make extra money.

Virtual Assistance. There are several small businesses who would love to have someone help them maintain and grow their business. There are several tasks that small business owners need help with, but they just don't have the time to do it themselves. That's created a huge opportunity for virtual assistants (VAs).

Some common tasks include: answering customer support emails, updating and maintaining websites, managing social media accounts, bookkeeping, transcribing audio, creating presentations and videos, optimizing websites for the search engines, sales, and many other simple and advanced tasks.

Web Shows. The rise of internet videos has resulted in web shows. You could produce your own show on the internet. Some sites, like Blip.tv for example, offer payment for your videos. The pay is based on how many times people view your video.

Like any job, it has its fair share of stress, but it also allows for a lot of freedom and creativity. In all likelihood, this venue would only produce some supplemental income rather than a primary income.

Blogging. Surprisingly, blogging can become a lucrative business. When you put up a blog on the internet about a popular topic, you can monetize it with paid advertising, sales of your own digital products, and commissions from affiliate products.

Your set-up costs are minimal. You can get started with a domain from Godaddy (about $10 per year) and free hosting at Blogger.com. You'll eventually want to get better hosting, but free is a good place to start.

As you can see, there are many opportunities to bring in extra income. Use your creativity and talents to devise your own income stream. Don't let the confines of your current job keep you from boosting your income elsewhere.

There's always something you can do for extra cash. All it takes is a commitment to do it and the discipline to follow through with your plans.

LET'S TAKE ACTION

1.   How much extra money do I need to satisfy my needs?

2.   What can I do to bring in more money?

3.   Can I turn my hobby into an extra income stream instead of a cash drain?

How?

4.   How can I use the internet to my advantage?

•   Be bold! Ask for a raise at work.

•   Put an ad in your local community newspaper offering your services – babysitting, handy-work, dog-walking, etc.

•   Explore online opportunities such as writing, virtual assistance, blogging and web shows.

AFFIRMATION: EXCITING OPPORTUNITIES ABUNDANTLY APPEAR IN MY LIFE

New opportunities surround me every day. All I need to do is recognize them and take the leap of faith. I have an abundance mindset that keeps my mind open to these new opportunities.

Each morning I greet the new day with excitement and anticipation. I give thanks for my blessings and wonder what good this day will bring. When I search for the good in my day, I often find beautiful, hidden gems.

Living in the moment helps me recognize new opportunities. When I focus on the present, regrets of the past and worries of the future simply cannot exist. I explore all options of the moment in my mind and take decisive action to seize those opportunities that can benefit me.

My abundance mindset includes a healthy optimism that brings me confidence and helps me get over any hurdles in my path. When challenges arise, I expect that there is a solution and I seek it out. I inevitably find it and continue happily toward my goal.

Today, "Seize the day!" is my mantra. My plan is to keep an eye out for those opportunities that I know, without a doubt, will appear and then go for them with all the gusto I've got!

- Do I expect that good things will happen to me each day?

- How can I make my mind more open to new possibilities?

- How can I encourage myself to take swift action on the opportunities I find?

SHOULD YOU REFINANCE YOUR MORTGAGE?

Refinancing your mortgage can be a smart move if the benefits you'll receive outweigh the drawbacks. Obtaining a mortgage with a lower interest rate or lower monthly payments can be very attractive and can even save you thousands of dollars over the course of the loan. On the other hand, there are fees involved in the switch.

WHAT IS REFINANCING?

To get a clear picture of the benefits available to you, it's helpful to know the process involved in refinancing your mortgage. Refinancing your mortgage consists of paying off the loan you currently have and taking out a new mortgage loan. Your current loan gets paid off in the refinance when you close on the new loan.

However, it's generally easier to obtain refinancing than it is to acquire a mortgage loan in the first place. Depending on the amount of equity you have in your home, it's possible to make the switch without coming up with any cash up front other than incidental expenses, such as a new appraisal or title insurance.

The closing costs, however, can all be rolled into the refinance.

Equity is the current value of the home minus what you still owe on it. Your equity increases each year as you make your mortgage payments and also from the increase in the value of the home.

For example, let's say you bought your home 5 years ago. The price of the home was $100,000, you put in a $20,000 deposit, and you took out an $80,000 loan.

If your home's value increased by $10,000 each year, it's now worth $150,000, five years later. In the meantime, perhaps you've paid $3,000 on the principal of your home by making your mortgage payments. (In the first few years most of your loan payments go toward the interest, rather than the principal.)

So, $150,000 minus $77,000 (what you still owe on the loan) = $73,000. You have $73,000 in equity on your home in this example. You started out with $20,000 in equity and, in 5 years, you've increased it to $73,000.

WHAT DOES EQUITY MEAN TO YOU?

Your equity is what gives you all kinds of choices in refinancing your home. The more equity you have as a percentage of the value of your home, the more advantages you have when you refinance.

For one thing, for refinancing the home in the example above, you're now searching for a mortgage loan for only 52% of the total value of the home, rather than the 80% you were looking for in the first place. This opens up a whole world of new lenders that would be willing to take on the risk of lending you the money.

Any time your equity is enough so that you're financing less than 70% of your home's value, it's much easier to find lenders that will compete for your business, even if your credit leaves a bit to be desired.

In addition to making it easier to find a lender with more attractive terms than your original mortgage, your equity can also make it possible for you to obtain a good chunk of cash, which you can use to pay off your high-interest debts or make a major purchase.

CASHING OUT YOUR EQUITY

When you receive cash along with your refinance, it's called "cashing out your equity." Keep in mind, however, that whatever equity you cash out in your refinancing process becomes part of the money you're borrowing with the new loan.

For instance, in our example above, you owe $77,000 on your current loan. When you refinance, your new loan may be closer to $87,000 if they roll the closing costs into the new loan. You won't "feel" the costs of the closing, because you won't have to pay them in cash, but they exist and get rolled into the new loan.

If you wanted to cash out some of your equity, but you still wanted to keep under the recommended 70% re-financing threshold, you would first figure 70% of your home's value. At a $150,000 value, you could finance up to $105,000. So let's say that the amount owing, plus the closing costs come to $87,000, ($77,000 is owed, plus $10,000 in closing costs), you could still cash out $18,000 and remain within your 70%. ($87,000 + $18,000 = $105,000)

If you have good credit, you could cash out even more of your equity and look for someone to finance 80% of the loan. This would give you another $15,000 in cash, but your new loan would be for $120,000 instead of the $77,000 you now have. Even with a lower interest rate, your mortgage payments would, in all likelihood, go up.

Refinancing your mortgage with an equity cash-out sometimes

makes financial sense, even if you'd be starting out on a new mortgage loan for a higher amount than your current loan. You can pay off higher-interest debts or use the funds to make a cash purchase, saving yourself the interest you'd have to pay on taking out a loan for the purchase.

As long as you've gotten advantageous terms on the new loan and the payment is easily within your budget, you may find that you're able to significantly raise your credit score, too. Paying off your current debts and making your

new mortgage payments on time will build some great credit! Plus, you no longer have to make multiple debt payments each month.

Even though starting over on your mortgage loan can seem disconcerting, if you set it up with the bi-weekly payment system, where you pay half the mortgage payment amount every two weeks, instead of the full payment amount once each month, you can still pay off this new mortgage in record time!

There are both pros and cons to refinancing your mortgage, so consider them very carefully:

PROS

You can lower your monthly payments.

You can lower your interest rate, saving you thousands of dollars in interest over the life of the loan.

You can change from a variable rate mortgage to a fixed rate mortgage.

You can cash out your equity:

Use the cash to pay off higher interest debts.

Consolidating your debts in this way means one monthly payment instead of many.

You can pay cash for a major purchase instead of taking out a higher interest loan.

You can raise your credit score.

You can receive some nice income tax deductions:

In the USA, if you itemize your deductions on Schedule A, you can deduct interest payments on your home's mortgage. Credit card interest is not tax deductible.

Essentially, by using your equity to pay off your credit cards and putting that debt into your home mortgage, you've lowered the interest you pay on your credit card debt while, at the same time, making it tax deductible.

CONS

You're starting over on your mortgage, so it may take you longer to pay it off than if you had not refinanced it.

Your mortgage debt will be larger than before the refinancing, due to closing costs and if you take out some cash.

Your monthly payments may be higher if you cash out some equity refinance.

With the new mortgage, you may be subject to early pay-off penalties if you wish to pay off a large portion in the near future.

So the question of whether you should refinance your home depends entirely on your particular financial situation. It could do you a lot of good or it might not be to your advantage. Your best option is to consult with a financial advisor who can review your own unique situation.

HOW TO GET STARTED

If you're considering refinancing your home, a mortgage broker can save you some time and trouble in finding a lender. You can usually get a good recommendation on a mortgage broker from a reputable real estate agent.

Your mortgage broker can work with you to find the most advantageous funding for your financial situation. Basically, you tell them what you're looking for in a refinance (lower interest rate, lower payments, or cash out) and they take care of the details.

MODIFYING YOUR CURRENT MORTGAGE LOAN

There are some situations in which refinancing your mortgage isn't an option. Unfortunately, with the recent downturn in the real estate market, many thousands of people have found themselves in an "upside down" situation with their mortgage.

If the value of your home has lowered since you first purchased it, you could owe more on your mortgage than the house is now worth. If this has happened to you, and you wish to obtain more advantageous terms on your mortgage, you might want to look into modifying your current mortgage loan with your current lender.

You may be able to lower the interest rate, your monthly payments, or even the principal on the loan by modifying it.

However, most lenders won't even consider a loan modification unless you're at least 30 days overdue on your payment. Then they may tell you they'll consider it, taking up the time right up to the day they foreclose on it.

So trying to get a loan modification can be challenging, but it can be done. If you have a regular income and your financial situation is such that you would have no trouble making your payments if they were only a bit lower, your lender may be willing to work with you.

If this is your situation, contact your lender to apply for a loan modification. Then keep in regular contact with them by phone and fax.

Contact the department heads for the various departments you work with as your application progresses.

Send faxes to the specific departments requesting regular updates.

Record your phone calls, if possible.

Write down the name of anyone you speak with, the date, and a summary of each conversation.

The internet has many resources that can provide you with valuable knowledge for working with your lender. Just do a Google search for "Mortgage Loan Modification" and do your research for the full details on the loan modification process and how you can work with your lender.

With good communication and knowledge of how to make the process go smoothly, your loan modification can be a success.

If you're not upside down on your mortgage loan and you've built up some equity in your house, it's usually in your best interest to look into refinancing your mortgage rather than trying to modify your loan. Generally, refinancing is less stressful and more successful than a loan modification. Plus, refinancing also has a host of other benefits you may enjoy.

LET'S TAKE ACTION

1.   Do I have a fixed or variable rate mortgage?

2.   Is the refinanced rate low enough to justify the switch?

3.   How much equity do I have in my home?

4.   How long will it take me to "pay off" the costs of refinancing and begin realizing my savings?

5.   Do I plan on staying in this home for long time?

6.   Am I looking for lower interest, lower payments or to cash out my equity?

7.   If I cash out my equity to pay off other debts, do I have the discipline to stay out of debt once my current debts are paid? What will I do with my credit cards?

•   Research the terms of your loan to see if it's worth shaking up the status quo.

•   Estimate your home's current value and determine if you have enough equity to give you some advantages with refinancing.

•   If you're considering refinancing your mortgage, meet with a reputable mortgage broker to discuss your situation.

•   After meeting with the broker, write down the pros and cons of refinancing your mortgage. This will help you make an informed decision to refinance or not.

AFFIRMATION: I MAKE DECISIONS WITH THE BIG PICTURE IN MIND

I keep my priorities and goals in clear view so that, regardless of the circumstances, I do what I know to be the right thing for me. Even if emotions run high in a disagreement or the distractions of the day try to take away my focus, I automatically think of the big picture.

I ask myself, "What is most important here?"

In a disagreement with someone I love, I go with the solution that best maintains a positive, loving relationship, because that is what is most important to me. Whether I am right or wrong about a trivial issue does not matter.

In business negotiations, I keep my primary goal in mind and my discussions open to any solution that works well for both of us. This solidifies a profitable business relationship.

Another question I ask myself in order to keep the big picture in mind is, "Will this make a difference 5 years from now?"

If a single issue can make a difference 5 years from now, I know that it is a matter of some importance to my life. Otherwise, I keep it in its proper perspective. Either way, I make decisions accordingly, letting my priorities guide me in my decision.

I use this strategy every day, even in seemingly small decisions. Keeping my priorities in mind allows me to choose to live life according to what is really important to me, rather than being blown willy-nilly by momentary distractions. As a result, I live a fulfilling life!

Today, I intend to keep the big picture in mind and I let my priorities - not distractions - guide me in my decisions.

1. Do I tend to forget what is most important to me in the emotions of the moment?

2. Have I clarified my priorities in my life?

3. How can I get in the habit of keeping the big picture in mind?

CHECKING YOUR CREDIT REPORT REGULARLY

In this day and age, it's incredibly important that you keep up to date on your credit report. Your credit score plays a vital role in many essential areas of your life, including loans, renting a home or apartment, mortgages, and even your job.

If you are in the United States, your credit score is determined by information gathered by three separate credit bureaus. These are Experian, Equifax, and TransUnion. As a consumer, you're entitled to one free credit report from each bureau every year. In addition, you may obtain a free credit report when you've been turned down for credit within the last 60 days.

These three American credit bureaus developed a central service to make it easy for you to obtain your free credit reports. Their website is at https://www.annualcreditreport.com.

Through this service, you can request that your credit reports be delivered to you online, by phone, or by mail.

WHAT'S IN YOUR CREDIT REPORT?

Your credit report contains:

•   Your name and any other names you've used

•   Current and previous addresses

•   Your record of payments on your credit cards and loans, including your mortgage

•   Public records such as bankruptcies, judgments, foreclosures, and car repossessions

•   Your credit limits on each of your credit cards or other lines of credit

•   How long you've had each type of credit

•   The balance due on each credit source

•   If you've defaulted on any of your financial contracts

•   Anything that was turned over to a collection agency, like outstanding bills

Most of the information stays on your credit report for three years.

However, serious events like bankruptcies and judgments can stay on your credit report for seven or twelve years, depending on the type of bankruptcy or if it was a judgment.

HOW DO YOU GET YOUR CREDIT SCORE?

Although you have access to a free credit report each year, currently the credit bureaus do not include your credit score in your report. They charge a small amount to provide you this information. When you request your report, you'll have an opportunity to purchase your score also, if you so desire.

Some credit monitoring services also provide your credit scores as part of their service. These companies charge a monthly fee for you to have constant access to your credit reports and scores and notify you of new activity on your credit reports. Such a service can alert you to any suspicious activity, like identity theft, which is an important concern these days.

You may want to consider such a service if it would make you feel more secure or if you're actively involved in working with the bureaus to get things corrected and raise your credit score. With the credit monitoring service, you'll be able to see that your changes are being taken care of.

WHAT IF THERE ARE ERRORS IN YOUR CREDIT REPORT?

In all likelihood, there are errors in your credit reports. In fact, this is more common than you may think. This is why it's important to check your reports regularly, at least once each year.

You may find addresses where you never lived, other people's credit cards, and even their bankruptcies and judgments. It is surprising how often another person has your exact same name and sometimes even the same birthday. This false information can take a serious toll on your credit score and make it very difficult for you to get a loan, car, cell phone, or even a new job.

Unfortunately, creditors tend to believe everything in your credit report whether it's true or not, so it's best to get the errors corrected before you need to get a loan or go job hunting.

If you find errors in your credit report, contact the bureau that's reporting the error and request that they correct it. For the most part, they'll contact the creditor and correct the information. In the case of certain disputes with creditors, you can also have it listed on your report that the case is disputed. You may also need to contact the creditor directly and have them correct the error.

Here are the sites where you can report errors on your credit reports:

For Equifax reports: http://www.investigate.equifax.com

For Experian reports: http://www.experian.com

For TransUnion reports: http://www.transunion.com

Checking your credit report regularly and getting any errors corrected in a timely manner will ensure that the information they're reporting about you is accurate.

It also helps you to be proactive in working to raise your credit score, which will bring you a plethora of benefits. We're going to discuss this in the next section.

LET'S TAKE ACTION

1.   Am I planning on taking out a loan or mortgage in the near future?

2.   When was the last time I checked my credit report?

3.   Is my credit score worth checking on a regular basis?

• Request your free credit report from each bureau.

• Report any errors you find and follow up on the corrections.

AFFIRMATION: MY POSSIBILITIES ARE ENDLESS.

Life is such an exciting journey! It is never static and boring, but alive with new possibilities each and every day. As I grow and learn, I find new ways to recognize and take advantage of the opportunities that come my way.

One way that I find new opportunities is by stepping outside my comfort zone. I now realize that such marvels are always there, just waiting for me to discover them. When I allow myself to try new things, I open myself up to the joys of discovery.

When I venture out into the world, I often discover new talents and strengths within me that I never knew existed. In developing them, I bring a whole world of new possibilities into my realm.

Stepping outside my comfort zone expands my limits. I never know how far I can go until I push myself a little farther, and then a little more. Expanding my limits also opens up new opportunities for me to pursue.

Meeting new people also brings new possibilities. Every person I meet brings their own set of experiences and strengths to the relationship, often providing me with a totally fresh perspective of life. I go out of my way to meet new people and bring this new richness into my life.

My possibilities are endless when I actively take action to discover them!

Today, I choose to open myself up to endless possibilities by stepping outside my comfort zone, expanding my limits, and meeting new people.

1.   What new possibilities have I discovered by stepping outside my comfort zone?

2.   How has meeting someone new brought richness into my life?

3.   Have I ever pushed myself past a limit I thought I had? How did it bring me new possibilities?

WHY A HIGH CREDIT SCORE IS IMPORTANT

Your credit score can have a major impact on your life. Of course, this impact could be positive or negative, depending on your credit score. The higher your score, the more benefits it brings you.

MORTGAGE

One of the most notable impacts that your credit score will have is determining what kind of mortgage you can qualify for and even if you can get one at all.

If you have a poor credit score, you may get less than desirable terms or be denied for a mortgage altogether. Or they may tell you that they can get you financing if you come up with 50% of the cost of the house in cash.

A higher credit score will enable you to qualify for lower interest rates and a lower down payment. A lower interest rate not only saves you money on your monthly payment, but over the course of the loan, it can mean a difference of many thousands of dollars to you.

You may be thinking that you'll just rent. While it's true that renting an apartment doesn't require a loan, they may run a credit check to make sure you're able to pay the rent. A poor credit score may even keep you from getting an apartment, leaving you with little in the way of housing options.

LOANS

Mortgages are essentially huge loans, so if your credit score impacts your mortgage, it stands to reason that it would also affect other loans such as student loans, car loans, or smaller bank loans. Not having access to these sources of money because of a poor credit score can make your life much more difficult than it needs to be.

The higher your credit score, the better chance you have of securing a reasonable loan when you need one.

In addition, many of the great deals you see advertised only apply to those with good credit. For example, you may see an ad for a great deal on a car with no down payment. When you get to the car dealership to take advantage of their offer, you find out that it's only available to those with a high credit score.

When you see WAC or OAC in small letters in an ad, it means "with approved credit" or "on approved credit".

The lower your credit score, the more you'll have to pay for many items that you need or desire.

CREDIT CARDS

While you'll continue to get "pre-approved" letters from credit card companies, the chances that they'll grant you credit drastically reduces if you have poor credit.

Your credit score will also determine your interest rate and credit limit. So essentially, if you want to go out and buy high end stuff with your credit card, you'll need good credit in order to get a suitable limit. They don't just hand out limitless cards willy nilly!

JOBS

If you have poor credit, it may be more difficult to get a job if the employer does a credit check.

The reasoning behind this is that people with good credit are less stressed and more in control of their life. They may also be more able to focus on their job. A person with poor credit might also be more likely to steal from the company to pay their bills, so why take the risk?

As ridiculous as this may sound, it's the reality of today's job market. It does, however, provide motivation to keep your credit in good standing. With a down economy and companies laying off employees left and right, you never know when you may be looking for a job. Plus, moving up to a better job is easier with a high credit score.

CELL PHONES

Even cell phone companies look into your credit history when you make a purchase. Like every other organization, they want to know that you can pay your bills on time.

If you're a fan of texting, tweeting, web surfing, or even old fashioned phone conversations, it's in your best interest to keep your credit score on the high end.

Your credit score seeps into so many areas of your life that it only makes sense to keep it as high as possible. A higher credit score saves you all kinds of money, brings you opportunities not available to those with low credit scores, and makes your life a lot easier.

LET'S TAKE ACTION

1.   Is splurging on cool stuff worth the stress a low credit score will cause later?

2.   How has my credit score affected my recent purchases?

3.   Would raising my credit score make my life easier?

•   Pay bills on time and in full whenever possible.

•   If you're tempted to skip a payment or pay it late, remember that your credit score has wide reaching ramifications: a good credit score is essential to getting your dream house, car or even a better job.

•   Make the commitment to take action to raise your credit score.

AFFIRMATION: MY ENERGY IS FOCUSED ON POSITIVE SOLUTIONS.

My energy is focused on positive solutions because I recognize the importance of continually moving forward. I know that being content with what I have and where I am going helps me achieve my goals.

I have let go of the need to list all that has gone wrong or might go wrong.

I plan ahead so I can be prepared, and I focus my time and energy on what I want to see happen. Then I lay out the steps I need to take in order to achieve my goals.

I recognize that others may see things differently than I do. I respect the advice of those older and more experienced than me, but I also realize that I have the best understanding of my own capabilities.

I use the experience of others as stepping-stones to my own success, but I let go of the idea that I need everyone to be enthusiastically behind me in order to move forward.

Because I have put careful thought and planning into my goals, I am confident that I am making wise choices and continue to forge on, regardless of whether or not people understand or agree with me.

I let go of the paralyzing effects of negativity and reach, instead, for the energizing empowerment of positive focus.

1. Do I focus on the positive aspects of challenging situations?

2. Do I give proper weight to the ideas and advice of others?

3. Do my actions prove that I believe in my goals and in my capabilities?

HOW TO RAISE YOUR CREDIT SCORE

There are so many variables that go into your credit score that pretty much everything you do in your financial life can affect it one way or another. With this in mind, let's look at how some simple actions can raise or lower your score.

Here are some things that will damage your credit score:

Applying for a credit card. The simple act of applying for a credit card can hurt your credit if you apply too frequently. If you apply for several cards at once, it'll do serious damage to your score.

Spacing your applications out over time does less damage at once, but it lengthens the time it takes you to build up your total credit limit. Having high limits with low usage helps your score, but brand new cards can also lower it.

Even though new cards can lower the score a bit, it still helps to build up your limits over a reasonable amount of time. The credit score boost you'll receive once these cards show a wise record of usage is more than the temporary cut from when each card is new.

Using your credit card. Another factor in your credit score is your credit to limit ratio. This is essentially the fraction of how much credit you've used compared to how much you have. So the more you use your card, the closer you get to your limit and the lower the score.

However, you have to use the card occasionally. You see, if you just let that credit card sit in your wallet untouched, the company that issued the card may cancel it due to lack of use.

For a higher score, use your cards every so often, but keep your usage to less than 25% of the total amount of credit available to you and pay them off on time.

Canceling your credit card. That's right. Basically, once you have a credit card, you need to keep it. A lot of people make the mistake of thinking that closing unnecessary credit accounts will help their score. This is incorrect. In fact, it will lower your credit score as it lowers your total credit limit and affects your "credit age," doing damage on two fronts.

It seems that regardless of which way you turn, you end up lowering your credit score, which just begs the question, "How am I supposed to get a high credit score when everything I do damages it?"

Fortunately, there are also specific actions you can take that will raise your score.

ACTIONS THAT RAISE YOUR CREDIT SCORE

The best way to raise your credit score is to pay off your current balances. This will widen the gap between your credit balance and your credit limit. While having cards clear of debt is nice, you'll want to use your cards enough to keep them active.

Each month, charge something to your card and then pay it off before the payment due date. This will build excellent credit without you having to pay any interest charges. As time goes on, the fact that you kept those accounts open for as long as you did will lean in your favor when calculating your credit score.

While keeping your balance all on one card may be convenient for you, it's actually better to spread the debt around to all of your cards. While the total will still be the same, this will reduce the balance on each card and that will work in your favor.

This also helps form a sort of "revolving door" of debt. If you set up the cards so that some are due early in the month and others are due around the middle, you can set up a system where there is always a balance on at least one card at any given moment. This will show creditors that you're willing to use your cards without going overboard, thus boosting your credit score.

Lastly, check your credit report at least once each year and make any necessary corrections. This will keep you informed of what's going into your credit reports and alert you to any suspicious activity.

Another strategy is to get your free report from a different bureau every 4 months. Alternating your reports in this way spaces it out to where you only request one from each bureau once each year, so they're all free, but you keep up with more current information.

LET'S TAKE ACTION

1.   Do I frequently apply for new credit cards?

2.   Have I been careful not to max out my credit cards?

3.   How can I improve my credit score?

•   If you can't pay off a balance, try to pay it down to less than 25% of your limit.

•   If you can't get it down to 25%, then pay MORE than the minimum charge as you work on it.

•   Use your cards frequently and pay off your charges each month.

•   Space out your applications for credit to reduce the negative impact on your credit score.

AFFIRMATION: IF I FEEL THAT I MAY STUMBLE, I CONSCIOUSLY DECIDE THAT I WILL NOT REVERT BACK TO OLD HABITS

I am the one primarily responsible for my own well-being, therefore, I pay attention to the signals that my mind and body send me. I am vigilant in keeping myself from renewing bad habits, especially in those times when it is tempting to slip.

I build and maintain close ties with others who are also genuinely attempting to become healthy. Because I have those relationships already in place, I know that I can call on them when I need an extra boost, just as they are free to call on me.

I learn from those who have already defeated similar problems. I take advantage of the wisdom and experience of those who have travelled this road ahead of me.

I also eliminate sources of negative energy from my life. Because I pay attention to my inner voice, I know which people and circumstances cause me to trip up. I make it a point to avoid these situations, going out of my way, if necessary, to steer clear of peers and places that drag me down.

I am clear about my purpose. I share my goals with other caring individuals, and I remind myself daily of the benefits of staying strong.

Because I am focused on the big picture and utilize all support I need, I know that I am strong enough to overcome old habits.

1.   Am I willing to sever ties with those who drag me down?

2.   Where can I find a group of like-minded people who can support me?

3.   Do I recognize the value of learning from those more experienced than myself?

INTERNATIONAL CREDIT SYSTEMS

While this money management course goes into great detail regarding the system of credit in the USA (as that is where the majority of my readers reside), other countries operate within their own unique credit system. However, the principles of managing your credit, such as paying your debts promptly, still apply regardless of which country you may call home.

In any country, lenders are particular about to whom they extend credit. Naturally, they want to ensure that any money they lend will be paid back in due time. It may be their business to lend money, but their profits are made when they receive it back with all due interest and fees.

With this being said, let's look at a few of the varieties of credit systems you may encounter.

CANADA

Here in Canada, we have a similar credit system to that in the USA, but there are some key differences.

We have 2 major credit bureaus:

Equifax Canada: http://www.equifax.ca

TransUnion   Canada:
http://www.transunion.ca/sites/ca/home_en.page

Canadians can request a free credit report as frequently as we like as long as the request is made in writing and the report is delivered by mail. Requesting a report has no impact on our credit score, although it is noted in reports. We also can submit a 100 word statement to be included in our credit reports.

Another difference is the length of time transactions and events remain on our credit reports. Most items stay on the reports for 6 years. In some areas of Canada, bankruptcies remain on the reports for 7 years unless you file 2 or more times. In this case, they both will show up on the credit report for 14 years.

The Financial Consumer Agency of Canada publishes a helpful booklet to help you navigate successfully through Canada's credit system and offers many helpful links for managing your debt in Canada. Their website is at: http://www.fcac.gc.ca/.

UNITED KINGDOM

The UK also has 3 major credit bureaus:

Equifax: http://www.equifax.co.uk

Experian: http://www.experian.co.uk

Callcredit: http://www.callcredit.co.uk

You can get a copy of your credit report from each of the credit bureaus each year for a very small fee.

In the UK, there are additional things that affect your credit score that might surprise you, for example, voting. Registering to vote can boost your score, while not registering to vote can lower it.

AUSTRALIA

Australia also has many complicated formulas for calculating your credit score. To access your credit reports in Australia, go to the websites of their 3 major credit bureaus:

Veda Advantage: http://www.mycreditfile.com.au

Dun and Bradstreet: http://www.dnb.com.au

Tasmanian Collection: http://www.tascol.com.au

INDIA

The Credit Information Bureau (India) Limited, or CIBIL, is the go-to place to find out about your credit in India. This bureau is a private partnership between banks, credit information service providers, credit card companies, and more. You can also purchase a copy of your credit report. Their website is at: http://www.cibil.com.

As you can see, even though they may have a slightly different credit reporting system, each country still has a way to determine your creditworthiness. No matter where you are, it's still important to manage your debt wisely for best results.

LET'S TAKE ACTION

1.   Do I manage my debts in such a way that I could establish good credit anywhere?

2.   What can I do to achieve greater success with my credit management?

•   Request your credit report, regardless of your home country, and correct any errors.

•   Make a plan for becoming more creditworthy and take action to follow your own advice.

AFFIRMATION: I CAN SEE MYSELF CROSSING THE FINISH LINE VICTORIOUSLY.

I know that I am a winner! I am sure of my success because I use effective strategies and tools to keep me motivated, pursuing my goals, until I claim my victory.

I set my goals and create action plans that set me up for success every time. I divide my goals into achievable tasks and then accomplish each task, one by one, through to the end.

If I need to invest time or money into preparing myself for my tasks, I do it happily, knowing that these preparations propel me toward the life of my dreams.

I make my goals a priority in my life and incorporate time in my schedule every single day to work on the things that lead me to victory. Knowing that each day puts me one step closer to reaching my goals brings me the motivation to forge ahead.

Failure is not an option! I know that sometimes there will be blocks in the road, but I actively seek solutions that can get me past them. I overcome my challenges and get right back on my success track.

If I feel even an inkling of self-doubt, I use my affirmations to wipe it out and replace it with confidence. If I fear a challenge, I replace my fear with the courage to meet the test head on.

I keep my passions burning with daily inspiration to stoke their fire. I use meditation to envision myself crossing the finish line and relishing my victory in all its glory.

Today, I plan to rekindle my passion to pursue my greatest goal, make an achievable action plan, and accomplish one task that puts me closer to success.

What is my greatest goal?

Have I made my action plan of achievable steps to get me there?

Am I facing a challenge? How can I overcome it?

PROTECTING YOUR IDENTITY

Identity theft has become a greater challenge than ever with the advances in technology. Unfortunately, there are several ways that your identity can be stolen and abused by the selfish and greedy.

While the methods to steal your identity are many, there are also some solid ways to prevent others from obtaining your vital information.

KEEPING YOUR IDENTITY SECURE

Follow these strategies to help keep your identity safe:

Be thorough when shredding your documents. Simply tearing them in half won't do. An inexpensive electronic shredder will save you time and help protect your personal data.

Shred all documents. Do you find yourself discarding your credit card bills or pre-approval letters without giving a second thought? While the credit card companies do what they can to ensure your privacy, it's still possible for someone to take your identity with the information available on each bill. Shred all mail that contains personal information.

Sprinkle and spread remains throughout the garbage. Much is made about how these identity thieves are willing to rummage through your garbage. When throwing away old statements, be sure to spread all the pieces of paper around to ensure minimal chance of reassembly.

Place a few pieces of paper at the bottom, add a layer or two of trash, and then put in more. You can even "sprinkle" the bills all over the bag and get them all mixed up with the rest of the garbage.

Also, add as much miscellaneous garbage to the bag as possible. The more they have to rummage through, the more secure your identity is.

Avoid suspicious emails. Email phishing is one of the most common ways for thieves to get your information. Most of the time, you can recognize it as the spam that it is. However, identity thieves have gotten better at hiding behind official labels.

Only open emails from people and businesses that you know and trust.

Avoid clicking on any links in your emails, particularly for banking sites or online stores you've shopped at. It's best to input known addresses into your browser and access websites manually rather than click a link in an email.

Keep your adware/anti-virus software up to date. One way that hackers can get your information is through spyware and viruses. Keep your software active and up to date to avoid this data theft.

Run a virus scan on your computer at least once or twice each week. If you spend a lot of time on the internet and browse many sites, it's a good idea to run a scan every day.

Regularly clear out all temporary files and your history and run disk cleanups to get rid of any junk that has accumulated on your hard drive.

Avoid putting personal information, like credit card or banking data, in emails that you send. Emails are a non-secure environment that can be easily hacked. If you need to send private information, put it into a locked PDF file and attach it to your email. Then give your reader the code to unlock it by phone, fax, or in person when you see them. Or just call it in, instead of emailing it.

Ensure you're on a secure site when giving personal information. A secure website will start with "https" instead of "http" and your lock icon at the bottom of your computer will appear.

LET'S TAKE ACTION

1.   Am I leaving myself open to identity theft in any way?

2.   Am I shredding documents enough so that someone can't piece them together later?

3.   How do I protect my identity online and keep it secure?

•   Ensure that your anti-virus software is updated to the latest version.

•   Set your virus scanning software to run regular scans automatically.

•   Delete all spam emails and be careful opening suspicious emails.

•   Shred all documents beyond recognition to ensure that thieves can't reassemble them.

AFFIRMATION: I TRUST MY ABILITY TO MAKE THE RIGHT DECISIONS

I trust my ability to make the right decisions because I have taken the time and effort to think clearly and surround myself with wise people.

I let go of the idea that I should automatically know the answer to everything. While I am unafraid of tackling a problem on my own, I am also aware that I am strongest as part of a community.

I am fully willing to assist those younger and less experienced than I, and so I am confident that my older and wiser peers are equally eager to help me. I take advantage of that, knowing that I can only be my best if I make use of the many resources at my disposal.

However, I may not always have access to guidance. In this case, I advise myself by recalling my past experiences.

I think about my goals and whether the situation at hand will assist me in reaching them or whether it will hinder me in some way.

I think about my energy level and skills and assess honestly whether I am capable of taking on the task. If I do decide to take it, I make it a point to be aware of my strengths and weaknesses and where I may need help.

Because I pay attention to the lessons I have learned from my past, and because I have a clear picture of where I am headed in the future, I know that I can make wise choices.

1.   Who can I consult when I need advice?

2.   Do I keep a clear picture of my goals in mind when making decisions?

3.   What have I learned from past experiences that I can apply to current decisions?

SUMMARY

We've discussed several personal finance topics, so as we come to the end, it's a good time to look back over all that was discussed and summarize the most important points of managing your money effectively.

BUDGETING

While budgeting sounds like a daunting task, really it's quite simple. All that's required is that you keep track of how much money you have, earn, and spend.

Most budgets divide expenses into two primary categories, fixed and variable. But we add a third called: non-essential expenses.

The fixed expenses remain the same from month to month, such as rent or a loan payment.

The variable expenses, like electricity and food, change from month to month. While the numbers change, you can still create a solid figure by averaging out the total purchases for each month.

The non-essential expenses, like excessive amounts of clothing or entertainment expenses, are often thought to be needs, when they're really wants that are unnecessary to lead a happy and healthy lifestyle.

If your expenses are greater than you're income, you'll need to find a way to earn more than you spend, whether it's through making more money, spending less, or a combination of the two.

SAVING MONEY

One of the best ways to maximize your income is to minimize your spending. Depending on where you shop, you have a variety of options when it comes to saving.

For grocery shopping, keep an eye out for coupons. You can often find coupons for items that you buy frequently. While one coupon may not do much, it can be a huge relief to the grocery bill when used en masse. The effect is expanded when some stores double the value of coupons to give you greater discounts.

For entertainment, search for used items as opposed to new ones. Many stores, including Amazon.com and eBay.com, offer the same products in good condition for a greatly reduced price. If you're a big collector of books, movies, or video games, this is a great way to cut that expense down, while satisfying your urge to buy things.

Find out if your favorite stores offer a preferred customer program. This can give you access to better sales, as well as gift certificates, that save you money on the things you were going to buy anyway.

THE POWER OF CHANGE

You may dismiss change as useless, but it's actually a powerful savings tool. Find a jar or container and empty your change into it each day. You'll be surprised at how quickly it adds up.

When cashing in your change, take them into the bank to save the counting fee from those machines at the supermarket.

The saving power of change is so apparent that some banks have tweaked the concept for their debit cards. Rather than put the change in a jar, they'll transfer the change to your savings account. Ask your bank if they offer this type of savings program.

Depending on the bank, they may also match a certain percentage, giving you an extra deposit every year. It rarely amounts to much, but everything helps. Why not boost your savings by using the card to buy things you were going to anyway?

Anytime your bank has a way to help you increase your savings, take advantage of it.

TIME IS ON YOUR SIDE

When it comes to long term saving (for things such as college or retirement), it's beneficial to use time to your advantage. In other words, the earlier you start the better. Not only does this give you a bigger window to earn the money you need, but the interest you earn will accumulate and increase as time goes on. This will make your money work for you to a much greater degree.

Most people in their 20's don't even consider their retirement. In fact, it would be a safe bet to say that retirement is one of the last things on their mind. However, that is the best time to start saving up so you can let your nest egg grow to its full potential. Even a few years will greatly affect the amount of money you would've earned in interest.

SEPARATION CAN RELIEVE ANXIETY

Most saving methods involve putting the money aside so you can't spend it. Indeed, "out of sight, out of mind" can be used to your advantage.

Whether it's a separate bank account, a different wallet, or even hiding the money in your sock drawer, putting the money in a place where you won't think about it is a great way to get into the saving habit.

Storing your money in a sock drawer or under your mattress is fine, but a bank account of some kind is a much better option. In addition to your deposits, you can make extra money in interest, which adds up over time. Not only that, but a bank account is secured. Here in Canada, they are insured up to $100,000.

There is no theft insurance on your sock drawer.

CREDIT CARDS CAN BE YOUR BEST FRIEND... OR YOUR WORST ENEMY

Credit cards are very convenient and grant you a lot of freedom, but with that freedom comes responsibility. If they're not handled wisely, credit cards can become a great liability.

Prepare yourself for credit cards by starting off with a debit card. You get the same sense of freedom while knowing the ramifications of running the card through the reader. This will give you the discipline needed to properly handle a credit card.

THE SCORE DOES MATTER

Your credit score can have wide reaching ramifications on your everyday life. Things that can be affected by a low credit score are:

Ability to get a mortgage

Ability to rent an apartment

Your interest rate on loans and credit cards

Your credit limit

Cell phone service

Finding a job

Acquiring insurance

Suffice it to say, a low credit score can be devastating to several facets of life. Keeping your credit in good condition will benefit you in all of these areas. Good credit can also save you a lot of money with lower rates on loans and can enable you to live in a better house or apartment.

DEBT MANAGEMENT

The best way to manage your debt is to start before you become overwhelmed. Pay off your credit cards in full every month and avoid just making the minimum payment.

Sooner or later, you'll find yourself with some kind of debt, whether it's through student loans, car loans, or a mortgage. There's no sense in adding to that with high credit card balances. When it comes to paying off your credit cards, the best way to get out of debt is to pay more than you use in any given month.

Target your highest interest cards first in order to get out of debt faster. In some cases, paying off the smallest balance is a great way to kick start the process and to eliminate a whole payment as well as a set of interest charges.

When you've paid off a credit card or loan, use the money that would've been used to pay that bill and put it towards another one. This will start a snowball effect that'll get you out of debt faster and save you money on interest charges.

Paying off debt will save you money by eliminating the interest charges, that way you can start saving for your short and long term goals.

MAKING EXTRA MONEY

The internet has provided a convenient way to make money on the side. Whether you're a writer or aspiring film maker, there are websites and small business owners that are offering to pay for your services. It usually isn't enough to make a living, but it can bring in a healthy chunk of change and make for a second job with no commute.

Selling items at flea markets or on websites, like Amazon or eBay, can bring in some extra income on a one-time or regular basis.

Offering your services can easily infuse another $1,000+ into your income each month.

BOOSTING YOUR CREDIT

Your credit score can be lowered by:

Applying for too many credit cards

Using your credit card and missing payments

Canceling your credit card

Not using your card and letting it sit idle

Looking at the list, it may seem like everything you do damages your credit score! All you really need to remember is to keep your balances low and to pay off as much of the bill as possible.

Rather than keeping all of the purchases on one card, try to spread it through all of your cards to keep the individual credit-to-limit ratios low.

Missing payments is a bad idea. It allows the debt to accumulate much faster and it also results in a never ending flood of phone calls. Missing even one payment can result in a much higher minimum payment and higher interest charges.

AVOID YOUR OWN IDENTITY CRISIS

Identity theft is becoming a more serious threat as technology advances. People will go to great lengths to get your money and it's important that you take precautions.

Shred all credit card bills or pre-approval notices before throwing them out. Make sure that they're ripped and torn beyond recognition and scatter them throughout the everyday garbage to ensure that no one tries to put the pieces back together.

When working online, ensure that your anti-spyware and anti-virus software is up to date. Avoid fishy emails and websites. When shopping online, be sure the site you use is safe and reliable.

SMALL TRANSACTIONS ADD UP

When using your credit card, be wary of small purchases. It's common to dismiss these charges as nothing while you continue to use the card repeatedly.

With big purchases, you have a sense of awareness that you don't have when buying a tank of gas or a sandwich for lunch.

Avoid that statement shock when you wonder how you could possibly have spent that much over the month … and your heart sinks as you recognize each and every $5 and $10 purchase.

The good news is that this works both ways. By setting aside a small amount of money every week into a savings account, it'll continue to grow and grow over time!

While being able to save large sums of money would be preferable for anyone, more often than not, it's not realistic. As long as you save what you can, you'll be on your way to a financially comfortable life.

WHAT YOU 'NEED' IS OFTEN JUST A 'WANT'

It's tough when you're in a store and see something you really want. You may convince yourself that you can "afford" it or that the money doesn't matter.

As an isolated incident, this mindset is usually pretty harmless, but it becomes a problem when this forms a pattern of behavior. Spending more than you pull in will put you on the fast track to a debt and stress crisis.

If you can put off the urge to buy stuff, you can discipline yourself to only buy things when you can afford them.

Smart financial management boils down to making more than you spend. If you can follow that one rule, you're ahead of the game!

Are my expenses greater than my income? If so, how can I cut my expenses and simultaneously boost my income?

Do I buy things because I need it, or because I want it?

What can I do to reduce my energy and food expenses?

What am I willing to do to reduce my non-essential purchases temporarily so I can afford my fixed and variable expenses?

Has my pocket change helped to boost my savings? How can I take my savings to the next level?

What can I do, today, to start saving for my children's college education and my retirement?

How can I reduce or eliminate the use of my credit cards until they are fully paid off?

Have I ever missed a payment for my credit card? If so, what can I do to prevent this from happening again?

What debt repayment strategy can I begin using to pay off any outstanding credit cards or loans?

10. How often do I engage in small sub-$10 transactions? How much have these purchases added up to this month?

11. What opportunities can I begin to pursue to make a little extra money each week? I.e. A second job, selling unused items, offering services.

12. Am I happy with my credit score? What can I do to increase it?

13. Is mortgage refinancing a viable option for me? If so, what will I do to investigate this further?

14. Is debt consolidation a viable option? If so, who can I contact to investigate this further?

15. What am I doing to prevent identity theft, online and offline?

IN CLOSING

Money management is an important part of life. Saying that money makes the world go around is an amusing overstatement, but there's some truth to it! To get the things that you want in life, you need money. Knowing how to handle your finances will make it much easier, while also leading to a more comfortable lifestyle.

Effectively managing your money is all about gaining the necessary skills, implementing the strategies, and exercising self-control. It may seem daunting at first, but once you get into the habit of saving, making, and managing your money, you'll enjoy the freedom from fear, stress, and worry!

www.ingramcontent.com/pod-product-compliance
Lightning Source LLC
Chambersburg PA
CBHW022112170526
45157CB00004B/1593